The Dur

*Tough Crimes: True Cases by
Top Canadian Criminal Lawyers*
Edited by C.D. Evans and Lorene Shyba

*Shrunk, Crime and Disorders of the Mind:
True Cases by Forensic Psychiatrists and Psychologists*
Edited by Drs. Lorene Shyba and J. Thomas Dalby

*More Tough Crimes: True Cases by
Canadian Lawyers and Judges*
Edited by William Trudell and Lorene Shyba

*Women in Criminal Justice: True Cases By and About
Canadian Women and the Law*
Edited by William Trudell and Lorene Shyba

Florence Kinrade: Lizzie Borden of the North
Written by Frank Jones

*Ross Mackay, The Saga of a Brilliant Criminal Lawyer:
And His Big Losses and
Bigger Wins in Court and in Life*
Written by Jack Batten

*Go Ahead and Shoot Me!
And Other True Cases About Ordinary Criminals*
Written by Doug Heckbert

*After the Force: True Cases and Investigations by
Law Enforcement Officers*
Edited by Det. Debbie J. Doyle (ret.)

*Pine Box Parole: The True Case of Terry Fitzsimmons
and the Quest to End
Solitary Confinement (upcoming)*
Written by John Hill

What They Say

"These humanized accounts written by experienced officers from various law enforcement agencies caused me to reflect upon my thirty years in policing. The emotions, frustrations, and challenges associated with maintaining composure in heart wrenching situations are shared in these stories. Many of us have been there and know exactly how it feels to console victims after a lengthy court process, following a next of kin notification, or in the midst of family violence investigations. The stories, clearly articulated in the book, reflect upon the peaks and valleys of a career in law enforcement. They enable reflection and celebration of lengthy careers. Details disclosed may be for the first time which is apparent by the emotions expressed by the authors."

—*Myra James, Retired Detective Hamilton Police Service; Past President, Ontario Women In Law Enforcement; Past Vice President, International Association of Women Police*

"However fervently storytellers of the entertainment industry attempt to truthfully and respectfully convey the reward and toll of a life in law enforcement, very few approach the heart swelling, heart stopping and heart breaking accounts authored by the very people who lived them. This book helps to remind how law enforcement officers do not simply 'retire'. These men and women shoulder their calling forever, some with greater ease than others."

— *Gregory Jbara, Actor, "DCPI Garrett Moore" on the CBS Police Drama BlueBloods*

What They Say

"Many people have a preconceived notion of the work of a police officer but do not understand the personal sacrifices, the mental anguish, the emotional toll, and the interpersonal changes the investigations have upon them. Police officers carry scars and memories which can have profound effects upon their relationships with loved ones and family, for life. This book provides a gut-wrenching account of the true inside work of a police officer, tells of the forfeiture of our innocence, and provides a glimpse into the distress and disbelief within our society as investigators help the victims. This book provides a rare, honest, and raw account of policing like no other."

— *Michael Elliott, President of the Edmonton Police Association, Former President of the Alberta Federation of Police Associations, and Director with the Canadian Police Association*

"What sets the stories apart in *After the Force* is that they are personal history, not just sound bites. These stories are being told entirely first-hand by investigators with on-the-ground knowledge. The observations, memories and feelings give these stories a strong and authentic voice because they are so deeply personal.."

—*Sherri Zickefoose, Crime Reporter*

"The reader of these interesting stories ... will recognize the humanness of their characters. We ask a lot and even expect perfection from officers when this is never possible. A true appreciation of their dedication and passion should be the result.

—*Dr. J. Thomas Dalby PhD R. Psych., ABN*

AFTER THE FORCE

TRUE CASES AND INVESTIGATIONS BY LAW ENFORCEMENT OFFICERS

AFTER THE FORCE

TRUE CASES AND INVESTIGATIONS BY

LAW ENFORCEMENT OFFICERS

Edited by

Detective Debbie J. Doyle (Ret.)

Foreword by Sherri Zickefoose

Afterword by Dr. J. Thomas Dalby

DURVILE IMPRINT OF DURVILE & UPROUTE BOOKS
CALGARY, ALBERTA, CANADA
DURVILE.COM

Durvile Publications Ltd.
DURVILE IMPRINT OF DURVILE AND UPROUTE BOOKS

Calgary, Alberta, Canada
www.durvile.com

Copyright © 2021 Durvile Publications
Authors retain copyright of their individual stories.

LIBRARY AND ARCHIVES CATALOGUING IN PUBLICATIONS DATA

After the Force
True Cases and Investigations by Law Enforcement Officers
Doyle, Debbie J. Editor

1. True Crimes | 2. Law Enforcement Officers
3. Canadian Police | 4. Biography

Book Eight in the True Cases Series
Series Editor, Lorene Shyba

ISBN: 978-1-988824-49-9 (print pbk) | ISBN: 978-1-988824-65-9 (e-book)
ISBN: 978-1-988824-66-6 (audiobook)

Cover design: Austin Andrews | Back cover photo Julian Hobson
Book design: Lorene Shyba

Durvile Publications would like to acknowledge the financial support of the Government of Canada through Canadian Heritage Canada Book Fund and the Government of Alberta, Alberta Media Fund.

Printed in Canada
First edition, first printing. 2021

We wish to acknowledge the ancestral and traditional lands of Indigenous Nations
all across Canada. They help us steward this land, as well as honour and celebrate this place.

The statements, views, and opinions contained in this publication are
solely those of the authors and not of the publisher. No one involved in this publication is
attempting to render advice. Neither the publisher nor the editor can be held responsible for errors,
accuracy, or currency of content; for the results of any action taken on the basis of the information in the book;
or consequences arising from the use of information contained herein.

All rights reserved. No part of this publication may be produced, stored in a retrieval
system or transmitted in any form or by any means without prior written consent.
Contact Durvile Publications Ltd. for details.

We wish to thank all
law enforcement officers,
both serving and retired,
for their service.

CONTENTS

■ ■ ■

Foreword, **Sherri Zickafoose**   xv

Introduction, **Debbie J. Doyle**   1

1. Revealing the Monsters   13
   Debbie J. Doyle

2. The Russian Mafia in Newfoundland   29
   Tony Walshe

3. Through the Lens   47
   Gwyneth Allin

4. The Dirty Little Secret of PTSD   61
   Stu Gillette

5. A Full-Circle Experience   77
   Sharon Bourque

6. A Little Girl Named Rose   87
   Neil Masson

7. The Thin Blue Line   95
   Elizabett Cordeiro
   Includes, "Jimmy's Nightmare," Jim Vaughn-Evans

8. Making "Those Women" Stop,   117
   JoAnn McCartney

CONTENTS

■ ■ ■

9. "There is No Law Against It, Constable"   131
   Ernie Louttit

10. The House with the Little Green Door   147
    Debbie McGreal-Dinning

11. Missing and Murdered Children   163
    David Wilton

12. Adventures on D Platoon
    Trish Haley   173

Includes Postscript to Trish's story, Marc Denis

13. First Female Sergeant-at-Arms   193
    Jackie Gordon

14. Theft of the Cape Spry   201
    Ron Pond

15. If You Help One, You Help Seven   217
    Val Hoglund

Afterword, **Dr. J. Thomas Dalby**   234

Acknowledgements, **Debbie J. Doyle**   242

AUTHORS AND THEIR STORIES

■ ■ ■

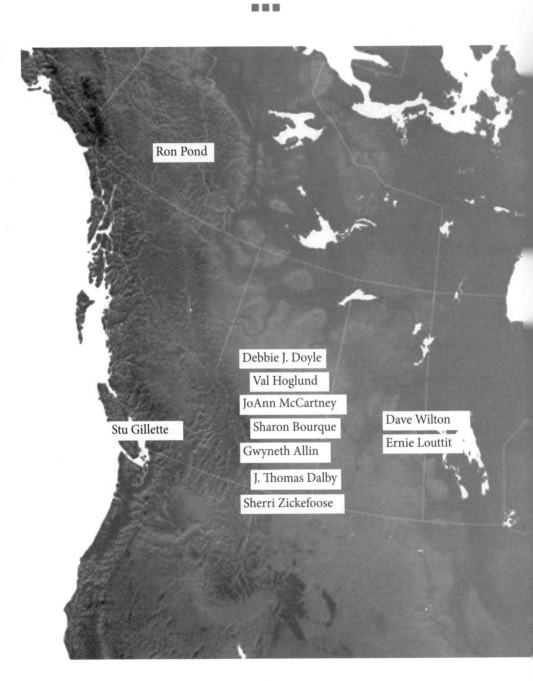

FROM ACROSS THE COUNTRY

■ ■ ■

Tony Walshe

Trish Haley
Marc Denis
Jackie Gordon
Deb McGreal-Dinning
Neil Masson
Elizabeth Cordeiro
Jim Vaughn-Evans

Ron Pond

FOREWORD

Sherri Zickafoose

There are far too many streets that bring back bad memories. As a crime reporter, my assignments covered every corner and beyond: an armed standoff, a fatal house fire, a riverbank where a rape victim was left for dead, a gang shooting, or the door of a home I nervously knocked on to ask a grieving mother or father questions about their dead child. This kind of lens changes the way you look at your city and your community. If this is reality after a twenty-year career as a journalist, what must it be like for police? The same goes for photographs of crime scenes and autopsies of murder victims. They are forever etched in memory from covering murder trials, but these were courtroom exhibits far removed from the raw incident. What lives on in the minds of the uniformed men and women who arrived at the scene with its horrific sights and smells, encountering people at their worst? How do they cope?

We want to learn more about what police are left with after facing off against the darker side of humanity. We are asking them to be vulnerable ... that is not easy.

These are the kinds of questions writers ask to humanize the subjects of our stories. We want to learn more about what police are left with after facing off against the darker side of humanity. The questions are often met with guarded answers. Why do we want them to relive it? Why do we want to know so much about the inner minds of law enforcement? We're asking them to be vulnerable and to do that in front of a large audience is not easy. We think of policing professionals as impermeable; the heroes who keep our communities safe and protect us from monsters. As civilians, we are left with a sense that only the inner circle of fellow members, trusted friends, and mental health therapists ever learn the truth about the terror, the horror, the close calls. But the questions linger: what are they most proud of? What is keeping them up at night? And how are they reconciling the two?

When Dr. Lorene Shyba reached out to introduce Detective Debbie J. Doyle, announcing her plans to edit and publish a book called 'After the Force: True Cases and Investigations by Law Enforcement Officers,' I was beyond curious and asked to learn more. Debbie's background as a former Edmonton Police Service detective gives her rarefied access to other retired members from across the country willing to contribute personal essays detailing their most haunting cases, investigative wins and reflective insights. Her experience as a distinguished 25-year policing veteran and as a United Nations peacekeeper gives her extraordinary insight into the life and death stories police live with. Her work persuading police to write about their most memorable cases and careers for readers outside the world of law enforcement undoubtedly came with challenges. Writing about something you really care about is a daunting task. Writing makes it real, and publishing it creates a permanent record. Hard-learned lessons can be humbling in the retelling. Reflecting on the lives they touched requires the writer to dig deep and confront painful memories or regrets. This kind of storytelling is passionate. It is powerful. And thanks to *After the Force*, it is very personal.

True crime is exploding within the entertainment industry. The public's appetite for podcasts, documentaries, and weekly television programming is limitless. This popular genre of storytelling piques our interest because we like to try solving puzzles and remind ourselves that we are safe from harm.

We want to learn more about what police are left with after facing off against the darker side of humanity. We are asking them to be vulnerable ... that is not easy.

From a true crime producer's point of view, it is considered a good 'get' to interview on the record an active or retired police member and put them to work retelling the tale. Police become characters in these productions helping push the narrative along. They are asked to break down memories of the crime scene, the investigation, and to share how these cases affected them personally. What sets the stories apart in *After the Force* is that they are personal history, not just sound bites. These stories are being told entirely first-hand by investigators with on-the-ground knowledge. The observations, memories and feelings give these stories a strong and authentic voice because they are so deeply personal.

We're curious to learn more about the stresses police encountered and what they are doing to cope because I think we have an impulse to try measuring ourselves against it; if they're struggling, what chance do we have to overcome trauma and sadness? But if they are thriving and resilient, it gives us hope. Through the stories offered in *After the Force*, that's exactly what we get. This insider view to the innermost thoughts of police is the kind of off-limits storytelling readers crave.

—*Sherri Zickefoose, Crime Reporter*
2021

Sherri Zickefoose is a former crime reporter for the Calgary Herald *and true crime co-author of the bestselling non-fiction book* Runaway Devil: How Forbidden Love Drove a 12-Year-Old to Murder Her Family *(McClelland & Stewart).*

This photograph of my back was taken by Gerry Meyers while I served in East Timor. He has since passed away and will be forever missed by his family, friends and those who his photography touched over the decades. —Debbie J. Doyle

INTRODUCTION

SUAI TIGER

■ ■ ■

Debbie J. Doyle

After the Force is a collection of chapters written by retired law-enforcement women and men who have come together to share their stories about defining moments of their careers, events that have affected them throughout their lives and into retirement. In recent years, many police agencies and officers in Canada, the US, and internationally have come under fire for unprofessional or unethical policing methods. This collection clearly displays another side to law enforcement; the human side.

This is the eighth book in the Durvile True Cases series with the majority of the first seven books featuring stories by and about lawyers, judges, and criminal justice. These previous books in the series were written after the incidents occurred and not from eye-witness accounts. *After the Force* is unique and intriguing in that stories are told from the perspective of first contact at crime scenes as observed by Canadian police officers who have served in municipal, provincial, and federal police services.

When I contacted the various retired officers, I wanted to ensure their stories were represented from across the country. These contributors served in small towns, remote areas and large cities, all having unique yet similar law-enforcement and retirement experiences. Among the themes presented were stories about prostitution and sex work, misogyny and racism, an encounter with a cop killer, police suicides, a child miraculously surviving a fall from a high-rise balcony, an officer dealing with a partner who was experiencing severe PTSD, a suicide from a bridge, and child sexual assaults. Most of these stories culminate with descriptions of second careers and new-found activities that have arisen in many of these officers' lives after retiring from police work, such as writing, painting, assisting Indigenous communities, and facilitating community improvement.

As for the title of the book, 'After The Force', many retired members refer to their career not by stating that they were law enforcement officers, but instead, shorten the terminology to being retired from 'The Force.' Back in the day, it was common to hear about a police 'force' being called out to respond to an emergency or deal with suspects. Now, we hear police organizations referred to as a police 'service', but sometimes old habits die hard. In retrospect, might I add, force is actually one of the least utilized parts of our job — instead communication and empathy are used in almost every interaction with members of the public.

Canadian Peacekeeping
Canadian law enforcement officers are some of the finest in the world. There are substantial differences between Canadian police officers and their counterparts in other countries, including our neighbours south of the 49th parallel. For example, we have in-depth screening and polygraph examinations as part of our hiring practices, and those who shouldn't serve are either not hired, or no longer serve. Police officers should not be feared, but respected by the communities they serve.

From having worked with officers from over forty different countries during my tours of duty in Timor-Leste, I have first-hand knowledge about the respect the world has for Canadian police officers. In 2002, I was seconded by the United Nations to serve on a peacekeeping mission in Timor-Leste (also known as East Timor), an island country in Southeast Asia, due north of Australia. While serving two tours of duty on the island, I saw time and again that people in charge of specialized units sought Canadian police officers with whom to work. The fundamental political and human rights guaranteed in *The Canadian Charter of Rights and Freedoms* is something people from many other countries can only dream about. Many countries limit or ban the freedom of religion, expression, and peaceful assembly. Freedom of the press and media is something, as Canadians, we take for granted. On many occasions, I spoke to the Timorese police and police officers from around the world about the legal rights set out in *The Charter*. I led by example, explaining that in a democratic country, police cannot arbitrarily stop individuals, cannot punish or torture people who are under arrest, and must remind people that they have a right to legal counsel.

The best way to explain the differences between Canada and Timor-Leste is to imagine stepping into a page of a *National Geographic* magazine that showcases a tribe of people who live in the jungle. Few people own vehicles. Walking or bicycling is the norm. Power is only found in the larger cities. Running water comes from a communal tap that families walk hours to and from on a daily basis. Heat? No furnace required. I have a photograph of a thermometer that displays 58.5 degrees C (137.3 degree F!). And bugs. Who knew cockroaches grew to be three inches long and could fly?! The first time I witnessed this, I saw a roach walking on the ground, until it decided to fly—at me! I'm sure the villagers thought I was being attacked by a saltwater crocodile — not my most glamorous get-away.

In Timor-Leste, villagers would routinely walk for hours to towns to report crimes at the police stations sprinkled around the island. When stationed in the town of Suai, I remember one incident in which a woman, Mrs. Ximenes, was the victim of domestic violence. She had walked to the police station to report an assault perpetrated on her by her husband—simply because his meal wasn't ready when he returned from working in the rice paddies. We initiated an investigation, obtained the evidence we required, and called the court in the capital city of Dili to determine when we could bring Mr. Ximenes before a judge. We drove Mrs. Ximenes back to her residence and informed her we would pick her up the following morning at seven. We told her we would drive her to Dili where she would testify and we would bring her back to Suai, if required.

After dealing with Mrs. Ximenes, we arrested her husband, took him to the police station and put him in jail overnight. In the morning, we picked up Mrs. Ximenes, put Mr. Ximenes in the vehicle with her, along with a translator and the Timorese police officers in charge of the investigation. To say the vehicle was crowded is an understatement.

The six-hour journey on partially paved roads, dirt trails, and goat paths required a stop for lunch. After I had given the Timorese police officers money to purchase food for everyone, we parked at the side of the dirt road, everyone climbed out of the vehicle and we ate while we talked. I had begun to learn Indonesian Bahasa when I first arrived and had a working knowledge of the language after several months (although when I spoke the Timorese would smile, probably thinking I sounded like a six-year-old).

Upon arriving in Dili, we went straight to court. The accused, Mr. Ximenes, the complainant Mrs. Ximenes, and the police officers all testified before a panel of three judges. Court proceedings with Mr. and Mrs. Ximenes proceeded pretty much as usual. More often than not in these cases of domestic violence, the accused is convicted but released back to live with the complainant, as was the case with the Ximeneses.

In court, both spouses signed a document similar to a cross between a Recognizance and a Peace Bond. A Recognizance is a form of release when an individual is charged with a crime, whereby the individual agrees to abide by all of the conditions as set out in the Recognizance. The most common conditions in a domestic violence case are to keep the peace and be of good behaviour and not to assault their spouse. A Peace Bond is a court order issued against an individual who has not yet committed a criminal offence, but an offence is likely to occur. In this case, if the accused does not assault his wife again within the year, he receives no punishment.

While Mr. and Mrs. Ximenes found places to stay with friends of friends or relatives, I spent my evening re-supplying food and much-desired beverages for myself and the officers I lived with. After all, on occasion, I too became thirsty. We only went to Dili once a month, so the time I was there needed to be put to good use. My husband Dan, who was stationed in another town on the island, took his re-supply the same day I went to Dili with the Ximeneses, so we met at Obrigado Barracks, a Portuguese military base. There, I ordered a large chocolate milkshake and my husband, an ice-cold beer.

In Suai, we had a generator, which we only used for a few hours every second evening, so I never purchased food that needed to be refrigerated. Therefore, in Dili, we ordered steaks—needless to say, they weren't Alberta beef, but the Australian beef substitute reminded us of home. Within four hours of eating, the milkshake would always exact its revenge on me—but it was worth it. With no power, milk was no longer a staple but instead something I had once a month, and as much as I still loved milk, it no longer loved me back. We rented a room for the evening and I had friends joke with me about having a monthly 'conjugal jungle visit' with my husband. Not that seeing my husband wasn't the highlight of the stay in Dili, but I sure did enjoy the air-conditioned room!

We all met up again the following morning at seven for the return journey, as planned. After we drove Mr. and Mrs. Ximenes to their house, we ensured Mr. Ximenes understood the conditions of his release. We informed Mrs. Ximenes if Mr. Ximenes didn't abide by the conditions, she could return to the police station to file a report and we would arrest Mr. Ximenes and return him to Dili to face the judges. I cannot say Mr. Ximenes never assaulted his wife again, but when we checked in on the family, no further issues arose.

I explained that in a democratic country—which Timor-Leste had become with the United Nations' assistance—people should never be afraid of the police.

One Timorese police officer asked why I didn't physically punish Mr. Ximenes. He had witnessed the Indonesian military perpetrating physical abuse on civilians. I explained that in a democratic country—which Timor-Leste had become with the United Nations' assistance—people should never be afraid of the police. It is the people who give the police power to ensure society is kept safe. I pointed out police aren't judges and therefore could not and should not punish anyone. Then I posed a question to him. "Who would benefit if I assaulted Mr. Ximenes? Mr. Ximenes? Mrs. Ximenes? Me? The community?" Unfortunately, the Timorese people were subjected to the abusive and corrupt behaviour perpetrated by Indonesian military, when under their control.

Canadian police officers are renowned for treating everyone equally, and I consistently promoted that reputation. When off duty in Timor-Leste, I associated with many of the police from other nations as well as the Timorese police. On Sundays after work, we'd go to the beach and swim in the ocean under guard of the New Zealand military who would ensure the saltwater crocodiles didn't have their own special Sunday feast. I have a large tattoo of a tiger's head on my back and when I wore my bathing suit, it was visible for all to behold; hence my nickname, Suai Tiger.

After returning to Canada from Timor-Leste, I was promoted to the Child Protection Section of the Edmonton Police Service. After 25 years of service, I retired and began writing books. Then, in March 2019, publisher Lorene Shyba and I were introduced to each other by author Richard Van Camp. After several conversations, Lorene proposed the idea of a book involving retired police officers, the impact that police work had on them, and how their experiences allowed them to flourish in their lives after policing. I found the idea compelling and agreed to contact officers from across the country and solicit chapters for this project.

Managing the Trauma from Police Work

God give me the serenity to accept things which cannot be changed; Give me courage to change things which must be changed; And the wisdom to distinguish one from the other.
—*Dr. Reinhold Niebuhr*

Many police officers have sayings they use in their emails or correspondence, or that they abide by. The Serenity Prayer, although used for addictions, is also used by police. There are so many things in police work that cannot be changed and to differentiate between them can be a complex and heart-breaking experience. Things that can and have been changed are shown in many of the stories in this book. In the evening of one's career, one can distinguish the difference. Wisdom comes with time and if we all stand together, civilians and police officers and look toward the horizon, we can find solutions to many of the problems that plague our society.

Connecting with the Authors
When I began connecting with fellow officers about the book, the majority of whom I didn't know, the conversations reminded me of chats I'd had with former partners and members of my squads. Regardless of where we had served, the camaraderie in our profession enabled us to easily relate to one another. We spoke about our careers, comical circumstances that had occurred to us, and the difficulties we had experienced. None of us regretted our policing career, even though we dealt with physical and psychological injuries from our chosen line of work. Each of us loved our careers because we joined the police to help others, often with our own self-interests taking a back seat to those of society.

As my colleagues' stories started to come in, I was not surprised to hear echoes of my own experiences from my fellow officers. In Stu Gillette's story, "The Dirty Little Secret of PTSD," he describes being stabbed with a junkie's dirty needle, just as I had been. Both of us experienced similar thoughts about how we would contract AIDS and die within months or a few years. We also dealt with individuals who were teetering on bridges and wanted to end their lives. Stu's story showcases the events surrounding one such incident, but his are not sterile words that he read from a book. They are written from a lived experience which explains to the reader everything that he was feeling throughout. This emotional encounter will leave you exhausted.

Consider your feelings when you drive past a prostitute. Are you judgemental? Do you want to hurl insults? Or do you look the other way and pretend not to see? — like most people do. "If I don't see it, it isn't real." I've heard that phrase far too many times. "Making 'Those Women' Stop, The Truth About Prostitution" is a story in the book written by JoAnn McCartney, who has dealt with prostitutes for the majority of her career in law enforcement and beyond. JoAnn has thirty years of experience regarding the exploitation and plight of women and her story discloses how the legal and social systems have turned a blind eye to this problem. Then, you will see what JoAnn has done to make things better.

How many times have we heard about miracles on television? Oh, in today's day and age, many of us don't call them that, or even want to be associated with religion. However, in Dave Wilton's heartfelt story called "A Little Girl Named Rose," one such miracle actually took place, changing Dave's life and making him contemplate everything that he believed in.

'Mafia'. We hear the word and think of many shows we've seen on television, almost entirely based on incidents within the United States. But, have any of you heard about the Russian Mafia taking a foothold in Canada? How about in the musical and fun-loving province of Newfoundland? In his story "The Russian Mafia in Newfoundland," Tony Walshe takes us for a walk through the in-depth workings of the organization and the crime he investigated.

What do you do if your friend is depressed? And then gets worse? Do you try to help? Do you attempt to understand the reason for their depression? How much time are you willing to invest and how far are you prepared to go to ensure that your friend doesn't depart this Earth by their own hand? The empathy and passion of

Elizabett Cordeiro shines through in "The Thin Blue Line" as the welfare of others outweighs her own. How many of us could be like her?

Some did ... Some didn't
Canadian policing is universal in the sense that police officers deal with similar calls, investigations and difficulties. Not all of whom I contacted contributed. After speaking with them, a couple of the officers realized they couldn't write about the investigations that changed their lives because they still struggled with their demons.

Several of the officers who contributed to this book suffer from Post Traumatic Stress Disorder (PTSD) on a daily basis, albeit some far worse than others. PTSD is not something to be ashamed of because it is a common hazard of policing. While engaging in phone and email conversations over several months, I determined that each of us has worked, volunteered, or engaged in hobbies as a way to manage the trauma from police work.

This book is an attempt to share the human side of police work and provide insight into the difficulties they face, not only in their own lives but also in the lives of members of society — often at the same time. Police officers engage with thousands, if not tens of thousands of individuals throughout their careers. These interactions range from stopping a vehicle for speeding, to dealing with a victim of spousal violence, to arresting an individual for the brutal rape and murder of a child. Each interaction with a member of the public impacts the officer, whether it is a positive or a negative experience.

Unlike other professions, police are called when bad things happen, whether there is a criminal act or a death. When a police officer attends a sudden death or makes a death notification, it affects them. Deeply. They may not cry on the outside, but they do weep on the inside. When sitting with a family member and listening to stories about the child or spouse who died in a vehicle collision, the officer experiences collateral trauma. Certain units within police services, including Child Abuse, ICE, and Crime Scene Investigations are considered 'high risk' units in which officers experience high levels of collateral trauma.

These experiences shape and mold us. Many of us have plans for retirement, while others are lost, wandering in the wilderness without direction. Some officers leave their police service on a Friday only to join another police-related organization on Monday. For a variety of reasons, those officers want to leave their job but aren't ready to leave the general profession. Others leave, never turning back or talking about their service, engaging in a completely different line of work. Some don't work at all; they may volunteer or help others in different ways.

This book showcases individuals from across the country. There are common ties among the stories because there are common ties among all police officers. I hope everyone reading this book realizes police are people, merely human, and without super-powers. We have dealt with adversity in our lives, we have made mistakes, and now we are all dealing with the effects of a career in police work, each in our own unique way. We all wanted to help people and still want to help by providing insight into these cases and into our lives and the way we have coped with our profession. We hope the sharing of our stories will bring readers an added perspective for a clearer understanding of our victories and failures, both during and after the force.

Debbie J. Doyle is a retired veteran of the Edmonton Police Service. During her career, she was seconded to the United Nations Peacekeeping Force in Timor-Leste (East Timor) and after serving two tours, she returned to Edmonton and worked in the Child Protection Section and the Internet Child Pornography section. Debbie and her husband Dan enjoy horseback riding, scuba diving, gardening and hunting. She currently writes novels and enjoys telling stories around campfires, sipping on her home-made crabapple liqueur.

1

REVEALING THE MONSTERS

■ ■ ■

Debbie J. Doyle

"**D**ADDY TOUCHED MY PEE-PEE." If that sentence doesn't make your heart race and your mind search for a response, what does? What do we say? What do we do?

Imagine you are Olivia, eight years old and about three feet tall. After everyone has left the classroom and only you and your favourite teacher remain, you tell your teacher that your dad touched your private parts. Your teacher listens to you, hugs you, and then calls the police. A large police officer meets you and takes you and your teacher to his police car and makes both of you sit in the back seat. It is recess, all of your friends are outside, and they can't help seeing you sitting there in the back of the police car. Your friends will think you are bad because police officers only put bad kids in police cars — everyone knows that. What will you tell your friends when you return to school the following day?

Further envision Olivia walking into the police station where all she sees are adults in uniform with red stripes on dark pants and a gun and handcuffs on their belts. The drab colours and smell of boot polish, floor polish and coffee swirl about and mix in your nostrils while your teacher holds your hand and walks with you into a room. You climb onto an adult chair in an office that has plaques and certificates on the walls. Not a hint of colour, only sterile and unfriendly.

A large man wearing a suit walks in and tells you he is a detective and takes you to another room — this one even worse. Four concrete walls, a desk and two chairs — and you're all alone! Your teacher isn't allowed to be with you.

When the detective talks to you, all you look at are his shiny shoes and dark socks. He asks you to tell him what happened. He wants you tell him about the first sexual experience of your life — not a consensual one, not an enjoyable one, but one that was unwanted, forced, painful, and upsetting. And what will you say? Or will you even talk to him?

As a point of contrast, imagine now you are Olivia, walking into an office where there are teddy-bears, bright colours, toys, people in normal clothes, and even dogs. This scenario is what Olivia sees at the Zebra Child Protection Centre, the first of its kind in Canada, in Edmonton, Alberta — a far cry from previous decades of police facilities in Edmonton, and light-years ahead of the system experienced on my tours of duty in Timor-Leste.

Innumerable Cases of Sexual Abuse
I cannot remember the number of cases I investigated and assisted with during my numerous years in the Child Protection Section at the Zebra Centre — a multi-disciplined unit where specially trained and dedicated members of the Edmonton Police Service, specialized assessors from Children's Services, civilian staff, volunteers, and medical professionals from Alberta Health Services work together for the best interest of children like Olivia. I don't mean any disrespect when I say that the multitude of child protection investigations blended together. Children were sexually abused, physically assaulted and forever changed, and regardless of what I did, I couldn't undo what they had endured —I couldn't take away their pain. I couldn't make them forget. But what I could do was investigate the allegations to the best of my ability.

Helping to set the stage for a child's comfort, the Zebra Centre interview room is painted in friendly colours, has curtains covering two walls, and is furnished with comfortable chairs. When interviewing children, I would sit on a cushion on the floor and a child such as Olivia would sit on the chair beside me, looking down at me. We would discuss the room and, on numerous occasions, I would be asked what was behind the curtains. Many of the children thought there were hidden window-mirrors, having seen them in police shows on television. They'd also ask about the object on the ceiling in the corner — the camera. Children are smart.

It never ceased to amaze me that within a short period of time, children would disclose the abuses that were inflicted upon them. In the majority of cases, it was by a family member or a friend of the family. In only a handful of cases the suspect was a complete stranger, unlike what movies portray. This made it difficult for the child.

While conducting any interview, rapport building is important, and frequently Olivia, or children like her would want to colour with me while we spoke. I remember coming home on numerous occasions after a long day, dejected. When my husband Dan asked why I was upset, I would explain that a child lectured me on the importance of staying within the lines when colouring pictures. But in fact, that was probably the best part of the day, earning the trust of a child and seeing them smile.

I mentioned before that many of the cases blended together, but I remember specific incidents that occurred in particular investigations. In one interview, I remember a young teen stating that when she was sexually abused there was a point where she experienced physical pleasure. She was devastated. In tears, she whispered, "My body betrayed me."

She was not the only one who disclosed similar feelings of guilt when during the assault, or repetition of assaults over days, months and even years, they experienced physical pleasure. Take a moment to let that thought permeate through the grey matter in your cranium. Then realize there are instances where the survivor cannot live with that guilt and takes their own life, even though police officers, counsellors and psychologists reassure them it isn't their fault. Did they commit suicide because they disclosed to us? How does this not affect a police officer?

Many of the older children declared that if they divulged what had occurred, it would become real and their life would change. They were right. Once a child discloses abuse, it is incumbent on an adult to protect that child and ensure the police are notified. Many younger teenagers know the repercussions of what a disclosure means. If it is their father, he would be forced to leave the home. If their mother knows about the sexual abuse and does nothing, thus condoning her husband's actions, the child is removed from the home, unable to see her father, and possibly not even her mother until the trial had concluded. And how long might that be? In many cases, more than a year, sometimes even two. Ponder that and remember the sacrifices you made by not seeing friends, family, children or grandchildren when Covid-19 arrived in Canada. A year to a child is a lifetime. They look upon the entire experience as a punishment because they are taken away from their home and from everything familiar.

After an interview at the Zebra Centre, kids would return to the playroom where their mother, father and/or siblings waited. Rarely was I allowed to leave before my partner and I were challenged to the competitive and favourite game at the Zebra Centre, 'Hungry, Hungry Hippo.' It never ceased to amaze me, that after such in-depth interviews, happiness enveloped the children, and when we played the game, their squeals of joy erupted when I lost.

Saturn, the God of Dissolution
As years transpire, so the soul blackens. Police and many first responders use dark humour to survive their professions. Time passes and day-to-day conversations involve more sarcasm, especially in high-stress units within the police service.

After our peacekeeping missions in Timor-Leste, Dan and I took my parents to Spain and Morocco where we visited the Prado Museum in Madrid, home to an extensive collection of works by the painter Francisco Goya. Goya's painting, *Saturn Devouring His Son* caught my eye so I purchased a print to keep in my office at the Zebra Centre. Not being child-friendly artwork, I placed it beside my computer monitor, out of sight to everyone except for me when I sat at my desk. I knew Goya had experienced mental anguish by the way he painted Saturn's eyes.

A colleague of mine asked, Why do you have that horrible picture in your office?" and I explained that we deal with the monsters certain men and women keep hidden deep inside of themselves, only to emerge when they abuse children. I further explained that it was our job to reveal the monster and bring the individual to justice.

I distinctly remember one investigation where a young girl disclosed that her father had sexually abused her. After interviewing the daughter and other individuals, I arrested the father and interviewed him. After charging him, I took him to cells where he went in front of a Justice of the Peace for a bail hearing.

The following day, I began to write my police report, and while doing so, I reviewed the accused's video interview. My jaw dropped. When I had questioned the accused in the interview room, he had flung his head back, his eyes wild and raging. At the time, I thought nothing of it, but while watching the video at my desk, it brought me to a complete stand-still. I paused the video, looked at it and then at the

Saturno devorando a su hijo, Saturn Devouring His Son by Francisco Goya. Museo del Prado, Madrid.

Goya painting right beside the monitor. Their appearance looked identical. For a moment, I thought I was hallucinating — did someone put something in my tea? Springing out of my chair, I grabbed a colleague and brought her back to my office and had her sit in my chair. She asked what I wanted and my hand motioned to the monitor. I watched her look at the image on the screen and then Goya's image of Saturn eating his son. Her jaw dropped too. The eyes, the expression, even the accused's hairstyle was similar to the painting. I was not seeing things, nor was I crazy. When my colleague left, I sat, looking back and forth at the images. They are seared in my memory forever.

Over the next several months of investigating cases, a few of us philosophized about justice and what it meant to adults compared to children. Children want to be believed. Adults want a pound of flesh. To many of us, swearing on a Bible is making an oath that cannot be broken. Unfortunately, for certain individuals who are charged with criminal offences, swearing on a Bible in court is not much different than ordering a coffee at Tim Hortons. It is a means to an end. How many times have I witnessed an accused lying on the stand? How many times have other police officers, lawyers, and witnesses watched in dismay while the accused tells lies on the stand? Being a Monty Python fan, I brought up the concept of how testifying would change completely if, when someone lies on the stand, a lightning bolt strikes them. Dark comments entered the conversation, with Python-esque humour. The consensus was that three, not five, lightning strikes would stop everyone from lying on the stand. The first accused who lies and is struck by lightning would be a victim from an act of nature. The second accused, perhaps a coincidence? The third? God is watching.

Early one morning when I arrived in my office, I discovered I had a subpoena to attend court. I looked at the name and instantly remembered the investigation; the court date was almost two years after the child's initial disclosure. It was Saturn's *Doppelgänger*. Even though this investigation had occurred in the mid 2000s, I distinctly remember what happened in court, but not to me. In fact, I don't remember my testimony, but that wasn't the important part of the court case.

Everyone had finished testifying and the accused was on the stand; he testified to dispute the child's disclosure. During his testimony, the accused's ex-wife, who was in the courtroom, approached Sarah, a volunteer from the Zebra Centre. The volunteers assist the prosecutor with the child in court preparation to lessen the child's stress of testifying. They also accompany the families to court and, when needed, bring an accredited police dog to sit with the child during their testimony. Imagine what a child experiences when she or he testifies after experiencing sexual atrocities. The ex-wife informed Sarah that the accused was lying on the stand; Sarah, in turn, notified the prosecutor. The prosecutor took a short adjournment to confirm the lie, and when the court re-convened, the information was presented to the judge. Once the trial was done, the accused was found guilty and sentenced.

To allege that an accused is lying on the stand is a serious allegation, but in this case, the ex-wife had irrefutable proof. The accused was unfavourably involved with the police and legal system for decades and may have grown accustomed to lying about his identity and age. When asked his age on the stand, without hesitation, he lied. In this particular case, the accused's ex-wife knew his birth year. This was a simple lie about something that didn't affect the case but effected his credibility on the stand. It was the closest thing to a lightning bolt I would ever see in my career. A coincidence? I don't believe in them.

The Internet Child Exploitation Unit
After seven years, I left the Zebra Centre. Through tears, I made the announcement of my imminent departure first to the volunteers I worked with — they had become part of my family — then to the rest of the staff. It was a difficult decision. In my heart though, I still needed to protect children so I went to the Internet Child Exploitation (ICE) Unit where I would investigate offences against children through the medium of the internet.

When conducting a child pornography investigation, warrants are obtained to seize computers and other electronic devices. Once a copy of the images on the seized computer is made, the investigating officer must look at the images and determine whether they fall under the classification of child pornography according to *The Criminal Code of Canada*. There is a meme on the internet that I copied, printed and hung in my office. It is of a black cat, ears back, eyes bulging, with a look of horror on its face, the caption stating, "What has been seen cannot be unseen." No one should ever have to watch videos or see images of adults sexually abusing children, but I thank all of the officers who are still in ICE units across the country, darkening their souls for the sake of the children.

While at Zebra, when an adult testified and there were no witnesses or physical evidence it became a 'he-said, she-said' trial and obtaining a conviction was slim to nil — except for lightning bolts. At ICE, when an adult possesses a thousand, or tens of thousands of photographs of adults engaging in sexual acts with children, it's difficult to dispute. The old adage is that a picture is worth a thousand words. Ten thousand images of child pornography are worth a substantial prison sentence.

After ten years of explicitly dealing with vulnerable individuals, I spent the last two years of my career in the Patrol Support team, working with a young partner and assisting the junior officers with their investigations. While there, the weight of despair lifted and the joy of working with young, eager officers, emerged.

Retirement from Police Work
After twenty-five years of police work, including two tours of duty working in Timor-Leste, Dan and I both decided to retire. There is more to life than police work. Unfortunately, so many police officers don't understand or realize this until it is too late. I was Debbie long before becoming an officer, and after retiring, I am still Debbie. My career was never my identity. But what was I going to do once I retired?

When Dan retired, he became involved in the Edmonton Police Service Veterans' Association and became president. During his tenure, serving EPS officers called him when they dealt with retired members. Struggling with Post Traumatic Stress Disorder (PTSD), these members had nowhere to turn. Unlike the RCMP, retired members of municipal police forces don't have medical, physical, or psychological support covered by the federal government. Falling through the cracks, many municipal vets suffer from PTSD, and without support, they sometimes feel suicide is the last plausible solution to their struggles. Dan developed the Veterans' Assistance Program Society (VAP) to help the vets, and when I retired, I joined the board of directors and I still serve on committees and volunteer as the website administrator.

The VAP was an easy transition since we have constantly volunteered for organizations during our career. My parents always instilled in me that regardless of what occurs in my life, no matter how bad it is, someone always has it worse. Therefore, they told me to take my talents and help others. I did this by playing music at funerals and for the Royal Canadian Legion at Remembrance Day celebrations. I remember when my dad was in the hospital, he was in good spirits, but I wanted to lift them higher. I brought my music books and played the piano at the hospital. I hadn't touched the piano in a long time, but when my fingers caressed the keys, it was akin to dancing with a lifelong partner. People stopped what they were doing, looked at me, and a few thanked me. An elderly man gently touched my shoulder, bent over and whispered that I was playing his wife's favourite song. A hint of light entered my soul that day.

I needed to volunteer more extensively and we discussed the organizations that were personally important to us. Many of our relatives were in the military; my grandfather fought in the Russian revolution, my other grandfather was in the Polish military, and my father-in-law served in WWII. Dan served in the Royal Canadian Navy, both of us served in the United Nations as peacekeepers, and our son served as a member of the Lord Strathcona's Horse regiment.

Unfortunately, many of the Canadian military men and women who return from serving suffer from PTSD. With help and support from Royal Canadian Legions across the country, we lose fewer of them to their unending battles with PTSD. Being part of something larger than oneself is an important human quality. Therefore, volunteering on a regular basis with the Royal Canadian Legion was a perfect fit.

Time is the most precious commodity we have. Dan and I enjoy gardening, riding horses, and spending time with our dogs and cats. On occasion, we travel to Bonaire to scuba dive, and I find peace underwater. This helps me heal, but I realize I still need to do more for others.

Taking Up Writing
When I was in school, I loved the writing assignments in English class, and eventually I began writing stories of my own. I grew up on an acreage close to where my grandparents homesteaded and I spent countless hours outside, creating stories and eventually writing them down. *Dungeons and*

Dragons games and *Star Trek* reruns spurred me to realize 'limits' was a word without meaning.

My stories stopped when I joined the police because I had limited time. When our son James was young, these stories re-emerged; not in writing, but in the spoken word. I told him tales of the plants, trees, and animals; our favourite was how the elk received their voices. But James grew up and the stories ended. Then, when our grandson Aedan was old enough, I began re-telling him the stories I once told his father. On occasion, Aedan would look at Dan and ask, "Grandpa, is that really true?" Perhaps I'm a bit rusty.

I decided I would write stories once again. Since I had written police reports for twenty-five years, albeit, factual, without opinion, and occasionally, quite monotonous, I knew that my imagination would return. I remember the stories I wrote when I was a child, unbiased and fresh but after 25 years of seeing the horrors of police work, seeing people commit suicide, holding the hand of victims of sexual assaults, getting stabbed by a junkie's dirty needle, being involved in a shooting, breaking my bones and tearing tendons and muscles, unbiased and fresh no longer danced in my mind. The innocence of my youth was lost forever, never to return. That part of me fell into the abyss, and no matter what I do, it can never be rescued.

The desire to write science fiction and fantasy was gone, however I decided to write what I knew, what I saw, what I was told and what I experienced. I sat down at my computer and looked at the photograph of the Gedachtniskirche on Kurfürstendamm in Berlin, which hangs above my computer. It reminds me of the horrors of war and compels me to write about good and evil within our society. For the next month, only coming out to make meals, eat, get a little fresh air, and spend time with the animals, I typed. In fact, I typed so much that certain letters on my keyboard stopped working. I had successfully broken my first keyboard, something

I never thought possible. Within a month of locking myself in my office, the manuscript was done. We went out to celebrate, Canadian style, and drove into town to Tim Hortons.

This fictional manuscript I wrote describes people I dealt with, investigations I heard about, those I was involved in, and situations I was part of. When I write about these occurrences, even though the work is fictional, it's based on actual events that still occur. I hope when people eventually read my book, they will contemplate the problems that plague our society and begin conversations. If we talk about the problems, together, we can create solutions.

Looking back, I realized that embedded in my manuscript are values that were instilled in me in my childhood, my teenage years, and through the rest of my life. Good and evil, right and wrong, the disparity between rich and poor, and other societal issues intertwined subtly throughout the story. I realize that the flawed characters are similar to me, to family members and friends. The characters struggle in life, akin to the rest of us.

Unfortunately, people may not know about certain issues in police work such as victims being kidnapped and used as sex slaves, often being drugged, as well as the biases and dangers members of the LGBTQ2+ community face. Most readers of my fiction will not have been exposed to these atrocities about which I write. The more that people are informed of the events happening around them, the more likely they will become involved to help solve this ubiquitous problem. I now comprehend that my writing will not only chip away at the soot on my soul, but will help enlighten others, and perhaps they too will help mankind, even if it is only one person at a time.

Difficult Transitions

My husband and I were at the grocery store some time ago when we met a friend who had retired from policing. We exchanged huge smiles and big hugs but on this occasion I knew my friend was struggling. I could see it in his eyes and hear it in his voice — his words concerned me. I knew he was having difficulty with his transition, so I told him a story...

When police officers are sworn in, we are given a pair of wings. Told to obey and uphold the law, we help people and make split-second judgments that effect people's lives. As officers, we fly above society watching out for citizens, swooping down to take care of them, stopping them from getting hurt. We fly during the day and at night, the night being important because society needs to feel safe in their homes while they sleep. When they need us to, we drive fast, kick open doors and arrest criminals, and for doing our job, the public and promoted ranks give us commendations and medals. Society idolizes us in books, TV shows, and movies. We love our wings and want to keep them forever, but some of us keep them too long. Then, when we retire, our wings are cut off and we forever lose our ability to fly. No longer can we look down at the public, protecting them and ensuring their safety. No longer does society look up to us. Instead, we look up at those who still have wings, admiring them and knowing that is what we once were but can never be again.

Many officers experience this feeling when they retire and countless numbers of them quickly seek employment in another law enforcement position. They don't want to lose their wings and many officers make every attempt to keep them as long as possible, but the longer they struggle to hold onto their wings, the more difficult it is to surrender them.

After telling my story, I saw tears well up in my friend's eyes. Society expects police to remain emotionless; we can never show anger or sadness. It's instilled in us — cops don't cry. I hugged my friend and pretended I didn't see his tears, even though he knew I did. He quickly composed himself during our embrace and when we stepped apart, he smiled.

"Thanks, Deb. I really needed to hear that."

Police are trained to be police officers but they are never trained to cease being police officers.

I have been asked how I transitioned so easily from police life to civilian life. There isn't a single action that allowed this to happen, but instead was a cumulation of many thoughts, ideas, and circumstances. Dan retired nine years before I did, thus allowing me to observe his transition. I saw his struggles and knew the pitfalls to avoid. Depending on each other and talking about our difficulties has enabled us to deal with the PTSD. Volunteering has created situations where we can enjoy people, laugh and tell jokes with them and forget about the negatives in life.

My writing has created an outlet where I can write about the horrors in society, but in a fictional setting that will allow readers to reflect on the biases and prejudices of others. My writing may even make some officers re-evaluate their ideas and stereotypes and look at their beliefs differently. All I hope is that if even one single person who reads one of my works wants to change a negative thing in their lives, I have succeeded. Is that not what we all want to do?

Oh, and the painting of Goya's Saturn still hangs in my kitchen, a constant reminder that monsters are still out there.

Anthony Joseph Walshe was born on September 11, 1963 in St Johns, Newfoundland. He grew up in Torbay and still resides there. He is interested in sports, and hockey is his passion. Tony is an outdoor enthusiast. He hunts moose, fishes for cod, and enjoys ski-dooing, biking, and hiking. His favourite accomplishment in policing is having served 25 years. Tony received the Exemplary Service Medal for his service.

2

FINDING THE RUSSIAN MAFIA IN NEWFOUNDLAND

■ ■ ■

Tony Walshe

I JOINED THE ROYAL NEWFOUNDLAND CONSTABULARY on April 1, 1985. After training, I was assigned to Patrol where officers go to learn the fundamentals of policing. I was assigned to the St. John's and Metro area of Newfoundland which consisted of half the population of Newfoundland. I worked in patrol until 1989 and then transferred to the Criminal Investigations Division.

I began investigating break and enters which was the entry-level investigation in this Division. Unfortunately, property crimes are common. When people leave their houses and go to work, criminals take advantage of their absence and break in. When people leave their work, criminals take advantage and break in to the businesses. It is a vicious cycle, and many people believe that breaking and entering is somewhat of a victimless crime because the insurance companies can cover the cost of the damages and the property that is stolen. However, if your residence has ever been broken into, you know those deep feelings of violation, insecurity, and loss. The trauma can be overwhelming. There are people who never feel safe in their homes again. Trying to solve these crimes is challenging if the perpetrators don't leave any evidence behind, making it difficult to catch them and prevent them from continuing with their crimes.

I took this job seriously because I wanted to ensure that the people who were broken into felt safe. Even if I couldn't determine who was responsible for the crime, I wanted to protect the victims and provide them with assistance on helping to prevent this from re-occurring. These types of investigations then expanded to include thefts of autos because vehicles were often used for break and enters and other crimes. After the crime, many of the vehicles were torched in an effort to ensure that police could not obtain any evidence. Thus, began my arson investigations, and this is where my first story begins.

Arson

It was winter of 1997, possibly in February, when I responded to a fire of a two-story residential home in the old part of St. John's, Newfoundland. The fire department was already there to put out the blaze, and now it was safe to enter. Arson investigations require a variety of expertise to investigate, and present at the scene was Cst Brad Butler of the Forensic Unit, Scott Tilley who was the electrical expert (also a fireman), a member of the Fire Commissioner's Office, and me. We worked as a team and were there to determine whether this was an 'accidental fire' or something more nefarious.

The role of the electrical expert was to determine whether an electrical issue was the cause of the fire. This was done for investigative purposes, which not only assisted with the police investigation, but also the insurance companies. The role of the Fire Commissioner's Office was to observe and deal with any fire safety violations — blocked exits, smoke detectors, building code violations, and so on. The member from the Forensic Unit was there to photograph the scene and seize, secure, and analyze the evidence. Being the lead investigator, it was my job to put everything together.

When I arrived, I smelled gasoline; that memory is still vivid over twenty years later. I walked through the house and observed burn patterns on the floor and multiple locations where fires had burned throughout the house, indicative of an accelerant being used. It wasn't difficult to tell the type of accelerant that was used because a red, five-gallon jerry can was left on the scene. I'm no Sherlock Holmes, but this was our first clue.

I was relieved that no one was home and that no one was injured in the blaze. We didn't know who the home owners were or whether it was a vacant house. During the investigation, I was standing on the front step of the house and noticed a lady in her mid-forties or fifties, walking down the street toward the residence. Since we were still investigating, there were marked police vehicles at the scene. The woman casually walked up to me, her dog affixed to the leash she was holding. However, it was not the woman or dog that struck me; it was the man with her. He was small in stature, had a slight build, coal-black hair, and a sad-looking face.

When the woman arrived at the steps, her first comment to me was, "Oh my God, I'm sure glad I got insurance." Now let's take a step back and think about that for a moment. If that was your house, what would your first comment be? Perhaps, "What happened? How badly is it damaged? Was anyone hurt?" There may have been comments about personal belongings. Might this be a second clue? Ah, the game's a-foot!

The woman told me that she was visiting family members in the Placentia area for the weekend. The area that she is talking about is roughly about one and a half hours away from St. John's. I took the initial report, obtaining basic information, including her name — Elizabeth Young — but noticed that the male who was with her stayed back and didn't interact with us. After she provided her details, they left and we continued with the investigation at the scene.

Unlike television, arson investigations can take weeks, even months, and during the course of the investigation, I noticed that the woman wasn't in a hurry to make a claim to the insurance company. Usually, people who have lost their homes due to fires contact their insurance companies immediately. Many insurance companies provide provisional money for hotels, food, and incidentals. We conducted interviews with Elizabeth Young and her boyfriend, Valari Sokolenko, the coal-haired man who was with her at the scene.

When I looked at his injuries they could have occurred around the time frame of the arson. The clues were dropping at my feet like flies being sprayed with Raid.

Both of their alibis about visiting at Elizabeth's relatives' house for the weekend were confirmed after we conducted interviews with her relatives. However, I knew that there was more to this investigation that what I was being told. I knew it was an arson, but I had yet to discover the reason for Elizabeth's house to be targeted.

Several weeks later, a man came to the police station and wanted to speak to the officer in charge of the arson. When I first saw him, I observed that he was burned; skin and cartilage had burned off his ears and nose and he also had burns on his hands. When I looked at his injuries and calculated the amount of time that they had healed, the injuries could have occurred around the time frame of the arson. The clues were dropping at my feet like flies being sprayed with Raid.

The individual, Vahram Kamalian, said that he had come from the hospital and that he needed to talk to me. I took him to an interview room and listened to his story. Vahram said that he was originally from Armenia and had moved to Canada. He informed me that he "owed" Serguei Lokhmachev, but wouldn't say what the debt was; Serguei was part of the Russian mafia. Serguei wanted Vahram to accompany him to a residence; Vahram believed that they were going to commit a break, enter, and theft. Believing that his debt would be paid if he assisted Serguei, Vahram whole-heartedly agreed.

At the time, VCRs, VHS movies, televisions, and jewellery were popular items to steal. People didn't record the serial numbers of the electronic equipment and movies weren't identifiable unless they were marked. Pawn brokers purchased stolen items and drug dealers accepted the items in payment for drugs. Jewellery was the easiest commodity to steal, transport and hide. The Russian mafia was known to work with jewelers who took the jewellery, removed the diamonds and gems, then melted the gold. Once melted, the property was untraceable.

During the late 1980s and early 1990s, the Soviet Union dissolved and tens of thousands of refugees fled to find a better life; many came to Canada. Montreal was the destination of choice and soon applications became backlogged. Newfoundland, however, soon became another desired destination because immigrants were processed quicker. Many members of the Russian mafia who arrived in Newfoundland eventually relocated to Montreal. Armenia and Russia had been in conflict over the centuries, and in Newfoundland, even though the eastern European population was smaller and they stayed together, the disputes from their homelands remained.

Russian mafia members were notorious for extorting Canadian Russians by threatening or injuring the families they left behind in Russia. Vahram explained that this was his concern and that's why he wanted to pay his debt to Serguei. I wondered how many immigrants were subjected to this type of extortion but never reported it to the police. I was disheartened to think that people who fled the former Soviet Union for safety reasons came to Canada only to be exploited by their fellow-countrymen. Unfortunately, this hasn't changed; today, we see it all over the world — human trafficking is rampant.

Then, without warning, a large explosion occurred; windows were shattered, flames were everywhere and his clothing was on fire.

Vahram said that Serguei drove him to the location in a van, and when they arrived and went into the house, he immediately smelled gasoline in the house. Ignoring his best instincts, he scrambled through the house, looking for items to steal. He noticed that Serguei wasn't with him but believed that Serguei was looking through different rooms in another part of the house. Then, without warning, a large explosion occurred; windows were shattered, flames were everywhere and his clothing was on fire. Realizing that he was caught in the blaze, Vahram raced out of the house, down the steps and onto the front lawn where he collapsed. When Serguei helped him into the van, he saw that Serguei was unharmed from the blaze.

Serguei drove Vahram to Harbour Grace, a small town on the Avalon peninsula about two hours northwest of St. John's. There, Serguei helped Vahram out of the van and onto a Lithuanian fishing vessel. Once aboard the boat, Serguei instructed Vahram that he had to remain there to await his return. Vahram told me that Serguei offered no medical assistance for him at all. His burns were painful, and when he first arrived, he was in shock. Unable to protest to any of Serguei's demands, Vahram spent several days sleeping, in between his bouts of what must have been crippling pain. During his semi-consciousness and then during his partial recovery, Vahram realized that the fishermen on board were not only fishermen, but his wardens. They were instructed to keep an eye on him and ensure that he never left the boat. When he begged them to allow him to go to the hospital for his injuries, they informed him he was not allowed to leave the boat and gave him aspirin for the pain.

Having worked as a police officer for years, particularly having investigated arsons and dealing with individuals who have been burned, I know that burns are incredibly painful. Many people would survive a second-degree burn, depending on the percentage of their body that was burned. Third-degree burns are much worse and have a higher mortality rate. And then there are fourth-degree burns which are horrific. All second and third-degree burns are extremely painful, and aspirin isn't generally the 'go-to' pain medication that is administered.

Vahram told me that while he remained on the boat, a man known as 'The Hitman', Oleg Velitchko, paid him a visit. Oleg was the second best kickboxer in the world when he defected to Canada from Russia. Oleg, told Vahram than he was supposed to remain on the boat as per Serguei's instructions, otherwise, he would suffer the consequences. Vahram, wasn't stupid; Serguei didn't want any doctors or nurses treating his injuries, becoming suspicious, and then notifying police.

While suffering under the supervision of his fishermen watchdogs, Vahram thought back and realized Serguei had already doused the house with gasoline before bringing him to the property — knowing when he lit the house on fire, Vahram would perish in the blaze. Serguei believed the police would have concluded Vahram was the arsonist and had died in the fire. No witnesses and no statements. After all, dead men tell no tales. Vahram, terrified of Oleg, remained on the boat for several weeks, but due to the immense amount of pain that wouldn't subside, he escaped to the hospital to receive treatment for his burns.

If Oleg returned, Vahram wouldn't survive the encounter — he was confident it would be his last. Therefore, he had no other option but to go to the police.

During his burn treatments, Vahram stayed with Tatiana Smirnova, who was also from the former Soviet Union. Off-hand, I cannot recollect how they knew each other, nonetheless, Vahram stayed with her for several nights. Tatiana lived in the area of Forest Road, which is close to the penitentiary in St. John's. While living with Tatiana, Vahram received a visit from Oleg. He was angry that Vahram left the boat, was determined to teach him a lesson and began assaulting him. Soon, a large donnybrook broke out and the police are called.

After Oleg's visit, Vahram's grasp of his situation became clear. If Oleg returned, Vahram wouldn't survive the encounter — he was confident it would be his last. Therefore, he had no other option but to go to the police.

Extortion and Threats

At the time back in 1997, it was difficult to believe that the Russian mafia was operating in Newfoundland; people thought that this type of criminal organization was only present in larger cities such as Vancouver, Edmonton, and Montreal, the latter being their main hub of operations in Canada.

At this stage of the investigation, armed with Vahram's statement, I now needed to determine why the Russian mafia wanted to burn down Elizabeth Young's house. Did Elizabeth owe Serguei money? Did Valari? It became clear we needed to conduct more interviews with both Elizabeth and Valari.

When I interviewed Valari, once again I noticed how small and frail he was; perhaps tipping the scales at 110 pounds. And his eyes — they were sad; he didn't have a bad bone in his body. Valari said that he was originally from Russia and his family still lived in Minsk.

After arriving in Canada, he eventually began dating Elizabeth. When Serguei approached him to extort money, Valari had nothing to give, therefore, Serguei threatened to injure Valari's family in Minsk. Valari said that he didn't know what to do and listened to Serguei's proposal. Unfamiliar with the operations of the Russian mafia, I was naive when Valari told me that Serguei would send a message to a contact in Minsk, who, in turn, would burn Valari's family's house down with them in it.

Serguei's plan was for Valari to take Elizabeth to her relatives for the weekend and stay with her there. Then, he would have someone burn the house down and Elizabeth could collect the insurance money. After she collected the money, she was to turn $25,000 over to Serguei. Valari, knowing that this would ensure his family's safety, agreed, especially since he wasn't required to commit the arson, only ensure that he and Elizabeth weren't there.

During the interview with Elizabeth, she said that the reason that Serguei extorted Valari was because she owned property and was dating him. She didn't want anything to happen to Valari, and she in turn, agreed to participate in the conspiracy.

It is difficult to interview individuals when they are terrified of speaking out against the people who threaten and commit crimes against them. Serguei and Oleg lived in the same community as Valari and Elizabeth. The Russian mafia was feared within this community, and being newcomers to Canada, their trust in the democratic policing system is little to non-existent. In many of their home countries, the police are either the enemy or are corrupt and cannot be trusted. Valari was terrified that since he told the police what had occurred, he or Elizabeth would be killed. During the interview and subsequent interviews with Valari, I reassured him that the police would protect him, even if it meant moving him to another city or province.

Looking back, the interview with Tatiana was the most interesting. I must clarify that statement; the actual interview was informative, but her attire was something that my colleagues still razz me about, over twenty years later. Tatiana was a young woman, tall, blonde, likely a model or had aspirations of becoming a model. She wore high heels, six inches or more, as if she wasn't tall enough, and a mink coat — definitely not regular witness interview attire. Through the interview and investigation, I knew that certain men exploited Tatiana, and whether that exploitation continued after the investigation, I cannot say.

In order to bring enough evidence against the Serguei and Oleg, we ensured that all of the witnesses were protected. Serguei and Oleg were arrested and charged and convicted of crimes including extortion, assault, and theft. Due to the severity of the crimes and the potential that they could flee the jurisdiction or threaten or kill the witnesses, they were remanded in custody.

Cases can take substantial time before they are presented in court, therefore, we relocated Elizabeth, Valari, and Vahram. Tatiana had contacts in Montreal and knew the owner of a restaurant and that she would be safe staying with him. She was flown to Montreal and remained there until she was required to testify in court.

Unfortunately, we were required to lay charges against Elizabeth and Valari as they were both involved in the crime. To me, Valari was the epitome of a victim who, without agreeing to commit this criminal offence, would have found himself, Elizabeth or his family dead; he was more concerned with his family than himself. All he wanted was to come to Canada and start a new life. I spoke to the prosecutor and discussed the possibility of Valari getting a lesser sentence because he was a victim. It bothered me that I had to charge him and I didn't want him spending time in jail because he was exploited; I believed it was my duty to help him.

Responsible Use of Force
This investigation remained in my thoughts even though I moved from Arson and transferred to several units before being assigned to the Training section. It would become an important basis for the direction of my career, both during and after the force.

I was assigned as the Use of Force coordinator in the mid-2000s; the term sounds overwhelming, and the amount of training to be done to ensure the safety of the members and the public is staggering. Police officers are required to keep current with their training and pass their firearms qualifications every year. It was my job to ensure everyone had completed their training within the time frame required. Officers were required to train in hand-to-hand combat, along with training with Oleoresin Capsicum (OC) spray (also more commonly known as pepper or bear spray), batons, tasers, and firearms. Television shows and movies glorify the use of these weapons; society, however, is often unaware of the extensive training involved before an officer is permitted to carry and use them.

I taught several modules over my tenure as the Use of Force coordinator. De-escalation through verbal communication is what officers engage in instinctively, often without even thinking. It becomes second nature. An officer speaks with everyone they interact with, whether it is the victim of a break and enter or the accused in a child sexual assault case. The way an officer speaks with an individual can affect that individual's behaviour and actions and impact our ability to get the information or resolution we need. It is an-important skill to master.

'Hand tactics' is another module where officers learn to use their hands to retain custody or ensure compliance when escorting or arresting individuals. This can range from soft-hand to hard-hand tactics. People may wonder about the importance of this for the officer or the suspect; this ensures the officer remains safe while dealing with a subject, but it also protects the subject from excessive force, too.

The use of OC spray, batons, and tasers are also taught. In the training, officers aren't merely taught how to use these weapons; they are required to know, according to the Use of Force model, when to use them as well.

Firearms training is the most in-depth of all of our training; as mentioned above, every officer is required to pass the qualifications, each year. If an officer does not qualify, they are no longer permitted to work on the street or possess a firearm. Our department, like other departments in Canada, take this training seriously. It was also during my tenure when we transitioned from the old 357 Ruger revolvers to the new and improved semi-automatic .40 calibre P226 Sig Sauer. The difference between the two weapons was stunning, and, not surprisingly, the training involved was extensive.

In Canada, when police officers use force, they are required to operate within the guidelines of the Use of Force model. This model categorizes all of the interactions with individuals from the cooperative subject to the active resistor to the individual who intends on inflicting grievous bodily harm or death. The tactics used range from the officer's presence to the use of physical control to the use of deadly force if need be. It's a heavy burden to carry. No officer sets out to kill perpetrators, but at times it regrettably becomes necessary.

Once officers use a weapon in the execution of their duties, they are required to document their use in a report. Part of my job was training officers to articulate the use of force in police reports so as to allow prosecutors and defence lawyers to read a clear and concise description of events. My position required the review of all Use of Force complaints that were made to Internal Affairs. In many cases, officers used less force that what the model allowed. Why? All officers are human, and none of us wants to hurt another human, especially using deadly force; it goes against everything we know, were taught, and believe in. It is a measure of last resort that no officer takes lightly.

Another module of training we covered was vehicle stops. The general public is unaware traffic stops are one of the deadliest interactions a police officer faces in the line of duty. They are always an unknown situation and pose a serious risk to an officer's safety. An officer might stop an individual because they observe a burned-out tail-light or an expired licence plate. The individual operating the vehicle, on the other hand, may have just finished a drug deal and have drugs in the vehicle. Or, they could have committed an armed robbery and still have the guns and money in the vehicle. There are any number of ways a 'routine' traffic stop can go sideways, and often quickly. The offender doesn't know why the police officer is stopping them, but, in their mind, they don't want to risk going to jail and they are willing to do almost anything to ensure escape. Unfortunately, while engaged in this book project, Sgt. Andrew Harnett of the Calgary Police Service was killed in the line of duty during a traffic stop. I cringe when I hear reporters calling them "routine traffic stops." Nothing, and I do mean nothing, is routine about a traffic stop. Nothing at all.

I cringe when I hear reporters calling them "routine traffic stops." Nothing, and I do mean nothing, is routine about a traffic stop. Nothing at all.

After working with the Training section for several years, I retired from the RNC in 2010. However, I was still a young man, at just 46. Throughout my life, I was always busy doing things. Even when I worked shifts, I coached minor hockey and spent a substantial amount of time with that organization, also volunteering for others. I didn't want to live idly. As luck would have it, prior to my retirement, a parent whose child I coached asked me to work in Fort McMurray, Alberta to conduct safety work — it was a perfect fit, being almost a continuation from the last several years of my police career, and so I accepted the position.

I began working for Canadian Industrial & Construction Training (CICT), a company dealing with Occupational

Health and Safety. After working with CICT, I soon realized non-policing jobs have similar issues, problems, and causes of injuries at their worksites as policing does. When working in the private sector, training workers about safety was also a difficult task. People don't want to be told what to do, especially when they think what they are doing is correct. In Newfoundland, many workers say, "That only happens on the mainland, not on our island." Accidents happen because people are in a hurry, often not paying attention, and they aren't working safely. In policework, we were told, "Complacency kills." That is not only true of policework, but in everything we do in life.

I will disclose a secret I've learned over the years working as a police officer and a safety consultant: 'time-worshiping' causes injuries. To some, that won't make sense; to others, it is as clear as the sky on a sunny day. The nature of people in our society is to rush. Everyone is in a hurry. We rush home from work to make supper and then rush to take our child to their hockey game or piano lessons — but, for what purpose? Always in a rush, we cut corners and become complacent to the task we are presently performing. As we rush home from work, instead of paying attention to our driving, the road in front of us, and the vehicles around us, we plan for supper; we wonder whether the hockey equipment has been packed or whether the music books are ready by the door. Speeding, red light violations, and collisions are some of the results of this complacency. Sometimes, people never make it home to their loved ones, all simply because they weren't engaged with what they were doing. They weren't being safe.

On construction sites, people are required to have specialized training on the equipment they operate, when they work at heights, or when they work underground. The training consists of instructions to perform the job, but it also consists of safety measures to employ while completing the job. When working at heights, there are certain safety guidelines that must be adhered to, otherwise people on the site could get hurt (or die), and members of the public who are near the site are also at risk. Why, then, would people not comply with the safety guidelines?! Because they want to save time. It may take several minutes to put on a safety harness and affix safety ropes, but since the individual hasn't been injured or ever had any close calls, they become complacent with their safety.

Qualifications for operating machinery, specialized training on job sites and safety gear are only a few things I've mentioned here, but there's always more to be taught and more to learn. I look at all of the courses in the private sector and policing sector and draw similarities among them. Our governments require training and certifications to ensure employees and the community stay safe. This is similar to policing, where the federal government allows police to use the equipment that they are qualified to use in order to ensure their safety and that of the public.

You may be wondering how, then, I can teach and reinforce this basic, yet most critical, issue. When teaching safety, I remind everyone: when they abide by the safety guidelines, they will go home at the end of the day to see their family and friends.

Safety
When I look back, I wonder why safety has become this deeply entrenched in my life and how it is connected to the arson of the house in St. John's. Regardless of the countless interviews I've conducted, the months of investigation, and the criminals I've charged, I was still required to charge Valari. That haunted me. I felt I had failed to help him, even when I spoke to the prosecutor about his cooperation with the investigation. I could not keep him safe. And through the years of policing, there were many other individuals

who I also couldn't keep safe; they died in highway collisions, fishing accidents, and accidents around the home. Needlessly.

From this reflection, deep down inside I realized it was the helpless feeling I had when investigating situations that need not have happened, and that this was the reason for me transferring to the Training section. It allowed me to ensure my fellow officers and members of the community remained safe when dealing with the police. Safety training in the private sector is the same; I want everyone to leave work healthy, enabling them to make it home to their families.

Time is on our side. All we need to do is take a moment to realize that life is too short to rush to our deaths. Take a deep breath, smell the salty air of the ocean and listen to the calls of the gulls above. This is what life is about; cherishing the simple pleasures.

Gwyneth Allin was a Police Officer for 30 years; last assigned to a Threat Assessment Team for a Criminal Intelligence Unit with the Calgary Police Service. She had the privilege to work in areas of the service that included Diversity Resources, Major Crimes, as well as Witness and Source Protection. During her tenure in Major Crimes, Gwyneth was designated as the Subject Matter Specialist in Domestic Violence, Criminal Harassment and Stalking. From 2007 until 2012, Gwyneth was a Threat Assessment Specialist assigned to an Integrated Threat and Risk Assessment Centre in Alberta. She has been qualified as an expert in threat assessment in both Provincial Court and Court of Queen's Bench in Alberta. Since her 2019 (semi) retirement, Gwyneth has been working as a civilian member of the Tsuut'ina First Nation Police Service and enjoying every moment as it comes!

3

LEONE, DARLENE, TAMARA, NAOMI, THROUGH THE LENS

■ ■ ■

Gwyneth Allin

"My first name is Gwyneth, just like Gwyneth Paltrow; you might notice the resemblance? Okay, perhaps you don't." That's my opening line, what's yours? Have you ever been asked to look back over your life or career and reflect on why you are doing what you are doing in retirement? For me, the pivotal memories, survivors I have worked with, and of course my quips, have been the building blocks that have tied it all together.

I always wanted to be a schoolteacher but in 1989, at the age of twenty-eight, I found myself in a police recruit class with twenty-seven other wide-eyed, fresh-faced officers-to-be. What had I gotten myself into?

In my thirty years of policing, I spent the first ten years 'on the streets' in the mud, the blood, and the beer, as my recruit class drill sergeant would say. I was in my fair share of bar fights — and then I went to work, of course.

In my time working as a front-line officer, I experienced many 'firsts'. One was to work undercover as a sex-trade worker. I remember my mom commenting that she didn't know if she liked the idea of me doing that work. I let her know that she didn't need to worry as there would be cover officers and that I could take care of myself. She replied, "Oh no dear, I know you can take care of yourself, I just don't like the idea of you standing out there in high heels for so many hours, that's hard on your back."

As time went on, I would share this quip, along with other stories, when presenting to hundreds of law enforcement officers, community members and other professionals in Canada, the USA, and Europe. The themes for which I became known were intimate-partner-violence, criminal harassment and stalking, as well as threat assessment and case management.

Another unique role I was privileged to take on was becoming the first liaison officer for the Persons with Disabilities Portfolio (including mental health) for my police service. Holding the position within the portfolio provided me with the opportunity to learn American Sign Language (ASL). As with many things in my personal and professional life, I have often found myself learning the hard way. Mastering a second language was no exception. During an ASL class, while practicing with another classmate, the instructor looked on as I proudly displayed my talent. What I intended to say was, "I want to go to the café for coffee." Expecting approval, I was taken aback when the instructor signed, "No!" I replied, "What?" It turned out I had said, "I want to go for a blowjob and a coffee." From that moment on, I knew I had to champion others to provide every person with the ability to hear and be heard by ensuring that a qualified interpreter was provided during an investigation.

Leone

Things shifted for me in the spring of 2000. My home phone rang. It was my mom calling to tell me that my cousin's 27-year-old daughter Leone had been murdered by her intimate partner. A few weeks later, I was sitting in a domestic violence training session as the trainers played a 911 audio recording of a child calling for help because his mother had been killed. My knees buckled and I left the room in tears. Leone's three young children had been in the home when she was stabbed to death. Looking back, I believe it was in that moment that I decided that I had to do something to try and prevent this kind of tragedy from happening to anyone else.

Darlene

After ten years as a first responder, I hit the ground running when I moved into the domestic violence unit. I joined my investigative partner Deb, who was already fully involved in cases that would change me as a police officer, and as a person. Most of what I learned about being an investigator and mentor to others, I gleaned from the survivors of intimate-partner violence, criminal harassment and stalking.

Darlene was one of those survivors. She had gone from one abusive relationship to the next, suffering brutal injuries and losing custody of her children as her story unfolded. Her first husband had slammed her head through the tile in their bathroom shower, causing her back to be split open from the base of her skull to her waist. She was subjected to death threats and criminal harassment. One such abuser used a box cutter to slice her vagina. He told her that if she was disfigured, no one else would want her and that he would "just use the other hole." Not every investigation associated with Darlene's circumstances resulted in charges being laid or proceeding through court. Darlene experienced anxiety, depression, substance abuse/dependency and had vulnerabilities that required a nuanced approach to ensuring her survival.

On one of the many trips taking Darlene to the hospital's psychiatric unit, I turned to her and asked her, "If you feel you must be in a relationship, why don't you try and find a 'nice' guy, rather than someone who hurts you?" Darlene looked at me and replied, "I have tried. But I get bored."

At first blush, one might think that Darlene was being flippant. What I realized in that moment was that what she was articulating, in her own words, was what her definition of 'normal' really was.

Many of us assume that to feel at peace we need calm surroundings and a feeling of being safe. Darlene's entire life had been filled with chaos, abuse and being anything but safe. So there it was. She only felt 'normal' when she was in crisis and chaos. She wasn't saying it was right, but she was being honest. Darlene taught me that it really wasn't about me or about what I wanted for her. From that day forward, I turned my mind to meeting each survivor where they were at, rather than where I assumed they should be.

My investigative partner and I were involved with Darlene for many years. We do not know how her life has been these many years later. I will admit that I think of her quite often, and I do hope she has found a new normal where she is safe and happy.

Tamara

Tamara is another amazing, brilliant, resilient woman who gave me yet another lens through which to look when dealing with survivors and intimate-partner abusers. Tamara is a survivor of one of Canada's most prolific criminal harassment and stalking abusers.

She had gone through years of trauma by the time we met, and I took over her case from the original investigators who laid charges against her former intimate partner, Jean-Guy Tremblay. In 1999, Jean-Guy Tremblay was convicted of assault, uttering threats, and unlawful confinement against Tamara. He had been previously convicted in relation to numerous attacks on women; most were his former intimate partners. The Crown prosecutor made application for Tremblay to be given long-term offender status, which a judge granted.

During my time as the assigned agent for Tamara, I filtered all communications sent to her by the National Parole Board regarding his case. During temporary release, or other weekend passes, I made the determination as to whether the information needed to be shared with Tamara. Tremblay was incarcerated in another jurisdiction, and allowing Tamara to be free from repeated reminders about the person who had caused her such pain and suffering was my top priority, along with ensuring her safety. As time passed, Tamara became a champion for change and decided she wanted to help others. Watching her strength, passion and determination inspired me.

In 2010, Tamara allowed me to facilitate her participation in research conducted by then-doctoral candidate Alana Cook who authored an article in 2014 along with Ashley Murray, Stephen Hart, and myself. The article detailed Tremblay's abuse against Tamara (Known as 'TM' in the article).[1]:

> In November 1998, while still on bail for outstanding charges, Tremblay met TM. TM was a 26-year-old single mother; Tremblay was 35 years old at the time. TM had recently moved from a small town in Alberta to the city of Calgary to work as an airline customer service agent. In November 1998, TM went out to a club for a "night with the girls" (TM, personal communication, February 11, 2011). Tremblay approached TM and her friends in the club and introduced himself as "Giovanni Hanchuk," and claimed to be a professional hockey player. She reported that she and Tremblay "hit it off" (TM, personal communication, February

---

1. Cook, A. N., Murray, A. A., Amat, G., Hart, S. D. (2014). "Using structured professional judgment guidelines in threat assessment and management: Presentation, analysis, and formulation of a case of serial intimate partner violence." *Journal of Threat Assessment and Management*, 1(2), 67-86.

10, 2011), and within days she met him outside of the local professional hockey arena for their first date. Within 2 weeks of meeting TM, Tremblay moved in with her and her 2-year-old son. He told TM that he had nowhere to live because he was not getting along with his hockey trainer and that he was between hockey contracts. TM thought he was moving in only temporarily. Tremblay arrived at TM's residence driving an old van stocked with only a can of molasses, a roll of toilet paper, and a portfolio of modeling photographs (TM, personal communication, Feb. 10, 2011).

Immediately after moving in, Tremblay began to engage in controlling behavior. For example, he did all of the cooking and would become angry if TM and her son did not finish their food. He also chose what TM watched on TV and would often watch shows at high volume at night so that TM could not sleep. He would not let TM shower alone. He insisted on bathing her. He would ration the amount of shaving cream she could use when she shaved her legs. He applied her make-up. He told her she could not hug her son. He changed her phone number and did not let her give the new number to anyone but her employer and her parents

Tremblay took away TM's keys and drove her to and from work. Once when she had to take a cab to work, he told her afterward that he had called the cab company to confirm the address at which she was dropped off. He called her repeatedly when she was at work. If she did not answer his calls, he left threatening voicemail messages or came to the office in person. When TM traveled for work, Tremblay called her hotel to confirm she had actually checked in (TM, personal communication, Feb. 10, 2011).

In addition to controlling behavior, Tremblay also

began to engage in IPV (Intimate Partner Violence) toward TM. The IPV started very soon after Tremblay moved in with TM, occurring at a frequency of about twice per week and comprising more than 20 separate physical assaults (Adams, 1999; TM, personal communication, February 10, 2011).

Tremblay jumped up and down "like a boxer" in front of TM and screamed, "Challenge me, bitch, just challenge me." Tremblay threatened TM with razor blades that he hid around the house and told her that he had a gun and that he had tried to kill another woman (Slobodian, 2000; TM, personal communication, February 10, 2011). Tremblay bought a Rottweiler, which he kept in the residence despite the fact that TM and her son feared the dog. Once when Tremblay was assaulting TM, the dog tried to protect TM, and Tremblay retaliated by physically attacking the dog (Slobodian, 2000). During other assaults, Tremblay punched TM in the ear and the groin, slammed a binder on her head, bent her backward over the sink in the kitchen and held her nose and mouth until her nose began to bleed, threw her against the walls, and threw her into the closet (Adams, 1999; Hainsworth, 1999; TM, personal communication, February 10, 2011). Tremblay even broke TM's wrist during one assault. When he took her to the hospital for treatment, doctors requested to speak with TM alone. Tremblay was enraged by the request and the couple was escorted out of the hospital by security (Adams, 1999; TM, personal communication, February 10, 2011). The IPV not only occurred in every room of TM's residence, it occurred outside of the residence. For example, Tremblay went to TM's workplace, closed and locked her office door, and beat her severely. TM's son was also victimized during the

IPV. Tremblay woke up the son in the middle of the night, straddled him, and screamed while he flicked the lights on and off. He laughed while TM's son cried in fear (TM, personal communication, Feb. 10, 2011).

TM told Tremblay several times that she was going to report the abuse. On these occasions, he threatened to kill her and then kill himself (Adams, 1999). He also threatened to kill her in front of her son if she told anyone about the abuse, and to kill her and her parents if she left him (Remington, 2000). Tremblay blamed the IPV on TM, saying she "made him" abuse her and that it was her job to calm him down; again she believed him (Adams, 1999; TM, personal communication, February 10, 2011). Tremblay refused to let TM use birth control and throughout their relationship was obsessed with getting her pregnant (Williams, 1999). In March 1999, Tremblay beat TM to the point that she could not speak or swallow and he allowed her to go to the doctor. While at the doctor she found out that she was pregnant; she was devastated and horrified by this news (TM, personal communication, February 10, 2011). Tremblay, on the other hand, was overjoyed and bought her flowers and a sympathy card, which he thought was an apology card, and promised her that the violence would end (Williams, 1999). She kept track of how many days passed without a beating after the pregnancy news; only 6 days passed before he assaulted her again (Slobodian, 2000).

TM tried to escape several times. She reported that she "got brave one day" (TM, personal communication, February 10, 2011) and went out onto the patio and screamed for someone to help her. Tremblay dragged her back into the doorway and beat her severely. Another time, according to TM, Tremblay had a "temper tantrum" and got out of the car during an argument. TM recalled thinking that this was her chance to escape, but felt bad for him and returned home to wait for him there (TM, personal communication, February 10, 2011).

The most serious assault occurred when Tremblay strangled TM to the point of unconsciousness and banged her head against a concrete surface. The assault occurred shortly after TM discovered Tremblay's true identity, including information about his previous relationship and court involvement with CD (Martin, 1999a; TM personal communication, February 10, 2011). TM received a package from her son's father containing numerous newspaper articles about Tremblay's history of assaultive behavior. The son's father had discovered Tremblay's identity and wanted to warn TM about him. She first confronted Tremblay with this information when they were at home. Tremblay was irate with her and bragged that he was the man who took [a previous woman] to Supreme Court in 1989. After this incident she did her own research about Tremblay and found more information about his past. She confronted him with this new information when he attended her work place. In response, he attempted to push TM down a parking lot stairwell outside of her workplace, but she caught her balance. When that failed he smashed her head into the concrete walls and strangled her. He forced her down several flights of stairs and said, "I'm going to kill you." TM thought she was going to die in the parking lot (TM personal communication, February 10, 2011; Williams, 1999, para. 6).

On March 19, 1999, Tremblay and TM attended a counseling session at his request so that she could learn how to act in a way that would not "piss him off" (TM, personal communication, February 10, 2011). TM disclosed the abuse to the counselor and Tremblay admitted to the abuse, bragging about the nature of the assaults (TM, personal communication, February 10, 2011). The counselor phoned the police and TM was brought to an emergency shelter for women (Slobodian, 2000). On March 21, 1999 the police went to arrest Tremblay. He slashed his own throat upon their arrival (Remington, 2000).

Eventually, Tamara joined with Dr. Cook and myself as we made presentations to service providers, law enforcement and others dedicated to assessing targeted risk for future violence and case management. On one occasion, Tamara shared her story with a large audience of highly skilled professionals. You could have heard a pin drop as she described the relentless, manipulative and horrifying treatment that she and her then two-year-old son were subjected to by Tremblay. It was as if you could hear the audience members thinking out loud, "Why would she stay in such an awful relationship? Why didn't she leave sooner?" Tamara paused after sharing her tragic story and then, as if she knew what they were thinking, she explained in a very quiet, yet confident voice, "To be completely honest with you, at the time, I had no experience dating a psychopath."

Tamara's ability to reflect on her own trauma, and ultimately reveal the raw truth about this type of intimate partner violence, allowed me to add another layer of understanding to the work that I was so passionate about. Intimate partner violence is a crime against society. The dynamics of this type of violence are complex. It is everyone's responsibility to have a fulsome understanding of the abuser's expert manipulative behaviour in order to expose the true nature of the offender.

Naomi

Then there was Naomi. Her abusive partner skilfully manipulated her, using all the trademark traits of someone who endeavoured to control his intimate partner. He moved in with her soon after they met, isolated her, checked up on her regularly, and used threats and physical violence towards her. Soon after their relationship began, Naomi became pregnant and eventually gave birth to her beautiful baby boy Cole. The abuse at the hands of Cole's father did not end after Cole was born. As time passed, Naomi tried her level best to make the relationship work; she wanted her son to have a mother and a father.

By the time Cole was two years old, the relationship had ended. Naomi, however, had allowed her ex-partner to stay in her home, in a separate bedroom, as he was unemployed and had not yet found another place to live. It was during that time that she experienced her intolerable event where she realized he was going to kill her.

She called the police; she reported what had happened to her. She went to the hospital to have her injuries documented; she worked with police investigators and went to family court to ensure that Cole's safety would be addressed by allowing his father supervised visits only. Naomi did not waiver, she would not return to the abusive relationship, and she would not allow her son to be exposed to the violence again.

Naomi's ex-partner was eventually granted unsupervised visits with Cole. On December 1, 2002, he failed to return Cole home to his mother. Instead, Cole's biological father made an incoherent phone call to Naomi then shot and killed his two-year-old son and then himself inside a truck on a rural Alberta road.

Naomi is one of the most resilient, amazing women I have ever had the privilege to know. At the time we met, I was training other law enforcement officers and service providers along with then-Crown prosecutor, Valerie Campbell, regarding domestic violence and criminal harassment/stalking. Naomi eventually volunteered to share her story, having a powerful impact on first responders and professionals with her candid approach. Although mistakes were made in response to Naomi's calls for help during her relationship, she did not shame nor blame anyone except her ex-partner. The lessons learned from her experience continue to have an impact on how law enforcement and the justice system view and approach complex intimate-partner violence situations. Naomi's willingness to share her story shed light on the need for specialized responses to intimate partner violence cases.

As my career wound down, I knew that I still wanted to contribute; but how? I had learned so many life lessons and wanted to share my knowledge with others. I had acquired skills doing threat assessment and case management, and truly still loved the work of policing.

As luck would have it, I was given the opportunity to contribute even into retirement; this time in a civilian capacity as a member of a First Nations Police Service. There is a subtle irony that has emerged as I enter my second year working for a police service within an Indigenous community. I once again find myself wide-eyed as I mentor others while learning, what seems to be, everything for the first time.

Despite having spent thirty years working in a major municipal police department, I was still naive enough to believe I had learned all there was to know. As it turns out, I am more often than not the student in my new role. Learning about our shared history, gaining insight into generational trauma, and having the opportunity to look at situations through a trauma informed policing lens has reinvigorated my sense of wonder and enhanced my desire to share what I am learning.

Leone, Darlene, Tamara, and Naomi will always be in my heart and I am eternally grateful for the lessons learned, despite the circumstances that brought their stories across my path.

This teacher will forever be a student.

Born and raised on Vancouver Island, British Columbia, Stu Gillette left high school early to work in the forest industry. He joined the RCMP Auxiliary in 1971 and determined that law enforcement was the direction he wanted to take. He joined the B.C. Fish and Wildlife Branch as a Conservation Officer in 1972 and then joined the Vancouver Police Department and served from 1975 until he retired in 2003. He currently resides with his wife Renee in Langley B.C. and is the proud father of two lovely, adult daughters, Kristen and Lauren.

4

THE DIRTY LITTLE SECRET OF PTSD

■ ■ ■

Stu Gillette

There is a lot of discussion these days in forums and on social media relating to police officers and Post Traumatic Stress Disorder (PTSD) . Recently, I saw an article that named this disorder as being "The Dirty Little Secret of Law Enforcement" — and it's not wrong.

I believe every police officer has felt the effects of PTSD to some degree and that the Dirty Little Secret has affected all of us, either directly or indirectly. What strikes me as most concerning is that these conversations are often written in third person, as if the troubling events happened to someone else and not to the author of the conversation. Could this be out of a misguided sense of shame?

Constable John Davidson, a member of the Abbottsford Police Department, was shot and killed in November 2017 while on routine patrol duty. The cold-blooded murder of a fine officer, loved by his family, colleagues and the community, brought the Lower Mainland population to a standstill. It was difficult to find anyone who was not grieving over this senseless act. When Chief Bob Rich gave his impassioned eulogy at Cst. John Davidson's funeral, I saw a lot of heads nodding in agreement and understanding. I also saw a lot of heads bow when Bob suggested to the police officers present, "It's time to take a knee and ask for help when you need it."

I agree with Bob, and I think it's time to drag 'The Dirty Little Secret' out into the open where we can fight it. With this in mind, I've written an account of certain events that have happened in my early days as a member of law enforcement. Some of these events are quite graphic, but the act of telling my tale is cathartic. My intention is to create a safe space for any of us who wish to tell our stories and, in doing so, maybe find some healing along the way. That is my hope anyway.

RCMP, Conservation Officer, and the Railway
Both my paternal grandfather and father were police officers. My grandfather began his career policing in England and after emigrating to Canada, he served for a short time with the Calgary Police Service. My father served as a military policeman with the Canadian Provost Corps during World War II, after which he joined the British Columbia Provincial Police (before its takeover by the RCMP). I was drawn to policing from an early age and, like many young Canadian boys, I dreamed of joining the RCMP.

In 1971, when I was 21 years old, I was offered an opportunity to join the ranks of the Royal Canadian Mounted Police Auxiliary in Nanaimo, B.C. Shortly after my swearing in, I was included in a series of training sessions and after a smattering of law, powers of arrest, and a brief stint at firearms training, I was released onto the unsuspecting public under the supervision and constant scrutiny of a regular member. Many times, I was reminded I was there to "Wave the Flag" and "Keep your ears and eyes open, and your mouth shut!"

After a time, a Non-Commissioned Officer (NCO) in charge of the program asked if I was interested in taking on a paid position as a Provost Driver. I would be issued a firearm and would transport prisoners from the various detachments on Vancouver Island to the Regional

Correction Centre in Victoria. It was interesting for a time but soon turned mundane with little chance of advancement toward my goal of becoming a regular member of the RCMP.

It was at this point in my career that one of my fellow auxiliaries, a Conservation Officer with the B.C. Fish and Wildlife Branch, approached me to ask if I would be interested in becoming a Conservation Officer (CO). I accepted and was sworn in as an auxiliary CO for the upcoming hunting season. Shortly after I assumed the part-time role, a fellow CO was transferred and so for the following year and through the next hunting season I temporarily took on regular full-time hours.

At the close of hunting season, I was in the office completing paperwork when the receptionist received a phone call regarding an unknown person having just shot a doe out of season. The caller gave the coordinates of the scene as the Northwest Bay Logging area near Parksville. I was dispatched from the office to investigate the complaint and got there about forty minutes later. The description of the scene provided by the caller was explicit and I had no trouble locating the site; it was up behind a large cedar stump, on a rise of land about fifteen feet above the road. As I climbed up to the stump, I observed a red vehicle parked across the ravine to my rear. I knew there was a well-travelled logging road on that side of the ravine, but the vehicle appeared to be purposefully hidden in a thicket.

As I reached to grab a branch to pull myself up, it broke and I immediately fell backwards. Simultaneously, a piece of the cedar stump exploded beside my head and covered my shoulder with chips of wood and dust. Almost immediately, I heard the report of a rifle shot and knew instantly I was the target. I dove to the ground and tried to make myself smaller, expecting another round to come my way. Instead, I heard the sound of a truck driving away at a high speed. I took a quick look, and sure enough it was the red pickup that had been hidden behind the trees. The truck had primer spots on the sides and front and I recognized it as one I had stopped on several previous occasions. The owner was well known as a poacher and local criminal.

I made my way back to my vehicle, tuned the VHF radio to the RCMP channel, and attempted to notify the local detachment of my situation. Unfortunately, I was too far out of range of the local repeater to have my call for assistance acknowledged and the vehicle got away. Subsequent searches at the suspect's residence were unsuccessful in locating him.

Approximately three hours later, Nanaimo Detachment received information that the vehicle had been involved in a head-on collision with a snowplow or a salt truck near Victoria and the lone occupant of the vehicle had been pronounced dead at the scene. A member of the RCMP investigated my complaint as a "suspicious circumstance — concluded here." I rolled that 'suspicious circumstance' around in my mind many times over the years and I still recall it with such clarity. The smell of red cedar can still educe the memory of that day's events. It was a surreal experience. The realization that another human being had shot at me with the intention of doing me harm or killing me was unsettling on a level I'd never felt before.

With the eventual hiring of a new permanent CO, my career prospects with B.C .Fish and Wildlife were not promising. I learned of a position within the B.C. Railway Police Department, stationed in the North Vancouver Detachment, and I applied. I was accepted and sworn in and measured for a uniform and kit. The role of a railway policeman is as far from exciting or stimulating as you can possibly get. Rattling doorknobs and checking freight sheds and boxcars loaded with liquor or electronics was the height of our daily excitement. Occasionally, a train would hit a vehicle at a crossing and the collision would need to be investigated to mitigate the railroad's liability, but that was as thrilling as it got.

A 'Piss Kid' at the Vancouver Police Department

I did not need convincing when I learned the Vancouver Police Department was actively seeking new recruits. I submitted my documents and after some written and physical testing, I was notified to join the academy class in 1975. Being a relatively junior member of a force staffed with World War II vets, 10-to-15-year veteran officers and a sprinkling of 'Piss Kids,' of which I was one, meant most shifts were spent under the watchful eye of one of the senior officers. Volunteering to attend radio calls and trying to get in on any interesting or exciting calls was frowned upon by the senior guys who had been there, done that, and no-longer-even-wanted the t-shirt. One-man cars operated by a junior officer were generally not seen sitting still very often, and any chance to patrol on my own was a rare occurrence to be relished whenever the opportunity presented itself.

Early in 1977 I was afforded that opportunity. I was assigned to work a night shift (2400-0800 hours) and staff a one-man car in one of the quiet sectors of Vancouver. The uniform members of the VPD Patrol Division had labelled District 4 'The Ponderosa' or 'Sleepy Hollow'.

In those days, the call load all but disappeared by one or two in the morning except on Friday and Saturday nights. The early morning hours were spent filling time however one could rattle doors or write tickets in order to maintain some level of interest and to stave off droopy-eye syndrome. Sunday graveyards were usually the most brutal and you half expected to see city workers out rolling up the sidewalks after midnight.

On this particular night, I had attended a couple of pretty routine calls: Break and Enter, Assistance to the

Fire Department, Theft from Auto, and a Motor Vehicle Accident. Things were starting to quiet down as we headed into the wee hours of Monday morning. To quiet things down further, the rain (what we call "The Greatest Policeman of All") was in full force, washing over the city as only rain can in Vancouver. It was one of those horrible, squishy nights where you swear the rain is coming down so hard it's bouncing back up and falling a second time, and it certainly wasn't the kind of night to get a call that required cops to stand out in the middle of the deluge in our spare-no-expense sponge jackets and leather-soled oxfords.

(To be fair, The City of Vancouver did issue us with reversible rain jackets. They were dark blue and fluorescent safety-orange, and they absorbed water at about half the rate of our standard patrol jackets. The absorbing qualities of the rainslickers were exceeded only by the shortness of the sleeves and the lack of any form of insulation.)

After completing a loop of the B.C. Police Academy buildings situated in the rear of the Seaforth Armories, I was sitting on West First Avenue at Burrard Street. A northbound car blew past me in a huge cloud of mist at 70 or 80 miles per hour. The speed of the car was so great and the water coming up all around it so profound I couldn't tell what colour the vehicle was, let alone the make or who occupied it.

My first thought upon witnessing this event was, "Oh boy. Car chase!" I pulled out onto Burrard Street and stomped on the accelerator so forcefully I thought I would dent the floorboards. I was probably approaching terminal acceleration on the old Ford Galaxy. Many police cars of that era didn't have electronic sirens, and I happened to have one of the older unmarked cars with a red, revolving 'bullet' dash light and an old klaxon siren (or fire truck siren) operated by flipping a switch on the dash and pressing the horn ring. The klaxon siren took so long to wind up and then wind back down you could get out of the police car, do whatever you had to do, and by the time you got back in the car it would still be whirring. The greatest downside to these sirens was that generally, you couldn't hear them over the sound of the engine.

I had my siren wound up to the highest pitch it could muster by the time I rounded the bend onto Burrard Street Bridge, en route to the downtown core, known as District 1. My training started to kick in and I remembered I had to switch radio channels from District 4 to District 1 and announce I was in a car chase. The radio was situated in the glove box and the mic was on the dashboard on a clip. As I reached for the radio to change channels, my hand knocked the mic off the clip causing it to tumble into the passenger side footwell. I couldn't reach the mic while also keeping my eyes on that fast-disappearing cloud of mist, now approaching Mach 1 as it hovered through the red light at Pacific Boulevard, so I made an instant decision. Informing the downtown troops of this pending danger was far more important than the momentary excitement I would experience from being in my first solo Vancouver car chase.

I stopped at Pacific and reacquired my communication equipment from the footwell in order to broadcast that an unknown vehicle was last seen heading northbound on Burrard Street from Davie Street at a high rate of speed. The chief dispatcher came onto the channel, requested a description of the vehicle, and asked if I was in pursuit. When I advised I had no further information and could no longer see the vehicle, I got the expected barrage of mic clicks and hoots over the radio. With my tail firmly tucked, I headed back to the relative safety of District 4. Or so I thought.

The Bridge

The rain was coming down even harder by this point, if at all possible, and I was beginning to think a '45' — what we call a meal break — would be appropriate as I pulled southbound onto the Burrard Bridge. As I approached the crest of the bridge, I saw a young woman walking south on the west sidewalk of the bridge. Seeing someone walking at two or three in the morning was not completely uncommon, but this young lady was wearing a tank top, jean cut-offs, and nothing else. Her hair was plastered to her head, and her clothing, what little there was of it, was soaked through. Of course, being a trained investigator with a natural sense of curiosity, I immediately determined this was out of the ordinary. Well done, Sherlock!

I pulled over to the curb, got out of the police car with the four-way lights flashing and began to approach the young lady who was about fifty yards from me. As I stepped up onto the curb in my blue and fluorescent safety-orange slicker, she recognized me as a cop and started to climb up onto the railing. I called out to her and tried to find something to say to prevent what I now feared was about to occur. The words didn't come easily; I stumbled, mumbling something about just wanting to talk to her and then begged her not to jump. The truth is, when I look back at it, I really didn't know whether to shit or wind my watch.

In times of intense stress brought on by fear and danger, the peripheral vision all but disappears and one can experience tunnel vision. I had experienced this phenomenon when the poacher shot at me some years before — it wasn't the exact same feeling, but it was pretty damn close. I remember the rain seemed to stop completely and we both appeared to be bathed in some kind of bright light, but everything outside of this brightness was pitch black. I don't remember hearing any sound other than this girl's voice, my heartbeat, and my breathing. As I took one more step toward her with my hands held out, she yelled, "It's in my back pocket!" and jumped.

Regardless of training, war stories from fellow officers, watching graphic movies, or any other gory or horrible life experiences, nothing prepares you for the blackness of that void, where only seconds before, a living, breathing human being stood, shining her light. It is utterly incomprehensible. The brain clicks into warp speed in an attempt to process the image and decide what to do next. Naturally, I pressed up to the rail and looked over the edge; I encountered a further shock that, in hindsight, I was totally unprepared for. The beautiful young lady who stood at the edge of her life just mere moments before was now a crumpled heap in the Aquatic Centre parking lot, in the middle of an expanding dark puddle.

The shock and horror of what just occurred had to be set aside because I knew I had a job to do. My radio was still on Channel 1 as I got back into my car and pulled a U-turn in the middle of the bridge to head down to the parking lot below. As I maneuvered down to the parking lot, I called the District 1 dispatcher, and in a high-pitched, cracking voice, I advised her to send an ambulance, a cover car, a supervisor, IDENT, and the Duty Officer. I probably asked for the fire department and street cleaners, too. I then told her, "Send everybody and notify the District 4 NCO too."

By the time my initial fear response lifted, I was on scene and had left the car to see if I could render any assistance to the girl. To my complete surprise, mixed with utter horror, she was still alive! She had landed on her face and her entire head was distorted and bent. She had an enucleated eye which rested upon her cheek and she was blowing bubbles in blood from her nose and mouth as she battled to breathe. I knew she must have sustained severe spinal and brain trauma and I knew enough not to move her in this state, but the human desire to help is sometimes overpowering. I felt a need to reach out to her somehow, to offer at least a minimal gesture of comfort. As I covered her hand with mine, I believe I felt her finger move as she exhaled for the last time.

The lingering memory of that moment is painful and many of the details remain vague. My vision and consciousness were still pegged squarely in the middle of that dark tunnel and very little existed outside of it. I was struck by how tiny she was. She looked as though she couldn't have been more than ten or eleven years old. I couldn't believe the blood in that huge, expanding puddle came from this one tiny girl. If I were to use one word to describe how I felt in that moment, it would be gobsmacked.

The cover car arrived first, just as I was standing up from the girl's side. The officers approached me on either side of my police car with guns drawn. One of the guys started shouting, "Is this the driver of the car? Why'd you shoot her? Where's the car? Do we need a dog? You didn't call for a dog!" I tried to explain she had jumped from the bridge and wasn't connected to the speeding car from earlier on, but I couldn't seem to get the words out of my mouth. As I stood there mumbling, one of the cover guys looked at me and said, "What the fuck is the matter with you, man?! Haven't you ever seen a dead body?"

The District 1 Sergeant arrived moments later, and I still owe him a giant thank-you for taking the two cover guys away from me. When the accompanying corporal asked me if she jumped, it was all I could do not to hug him and thank him. Until that moment, I felt as though I caused this horrible thing to have happened to this beautiful, vibrant young woman. Of course, I knew in my heart it was not my fault, but in the aftermath I immediately started to second guess every step leading up to her leap from the bridge and wondered what I could have and should have done differently to prevent this girl's suicide. Those self-speak/mind games are insidious. They still affect me now, but over time I eventually learned this is part of the process first responders often go through after suffering a traumatic experience in the line of duty.

I think everyone except the street cleaners eventually did arrive on the scene that night, and the young lass was taken away to the Vancouver General Hospital morgue to be processed by the coroner. Later that night, I found out what she'd meant when she said, "It's in my back pocket." Along with her identification and next-of-kin information in the pocket of her cut-offs was a suicide note. When I saw the note, I read it over and over, trying to find some understanding of what led to her decision to end her life.

The young lady was just 19 years old and one of a set of identical twins. Both she and her sister were dancers in a troupe from Edmonton and were dancing in a play in Vancouver. This girl was the lead dancer and her twin sister was the understudy. The producer or director of the dance troupe was in a relationship with this young lady and decided to break it off because he was actually in love with her twin sister. Not only did he spurn this girl's affection and break her heart, but he then relegated her to the part of understudy when he gave the leading part instead to her twin sister. That was all she could take, I suppose. She decided to end her life because, as she said in the note, "There's nothing worth living for. Sorry Dad!"

The last line of her suicide note is burned in my memory. I felt the reference to her father may have indicated a close relationship. I'm not sure if I was overreacting to the events of the night, but I felt it was incumbent upon me to do whatever I could to locate her father to let him know. I contacted the Edmonton Police Department and they managed to find her father. They conducted the notification and passed along my name and badge number. Her father and I never spoke directly, but he did send me a long letter thanking me for my efforts. Every year at Christmas, I would receive a Christmas card from him, sent in care of the Department. I think I got ten or so Christmas cards from him before they eventually stopped.

Like a Video Unfolding

To this day, the events of that night roll through my mind as if watching them unfold on video. This is a common symptom of PTSD, but thankfully it doesn't seem to incapacitate me. I don't break into cold sweats or exhibit any overtly negative behaviour. I don't know if I'm wired differently than others, perhaps making it somewhat easier for me to set the trauma aside, but the accumulated trauma has had a huge effect on my life nonetheless and the affects of the trauma will probably stay with me until I die. I've read keeping a journal or diary can be helpful, even if kept privately. I don't know about that. I don't know if I feel any differently than I did before I started this missive. I do know talking to someone about the trauma in your life is beneficial, and I would encourage all retired or serving police officers to "take a knee," as Bob Rich said, and "ask for help."

The years have flown by and the trauma I endured that night on the Burrard Bridge wasn't the last. I encountered many more tragedies over the course of my service. One or two of my experiences have resulted in counselling and considerable introspection. What was done? What could have been done? What should not have been done? Many of our decisions are often made in a split second, with limited information which is further clouded by angst and heavy emotion. Every situation, it seems, has a component of "shoulda, coulda, woulda" and I believe this rumination is what leads many of us into the dark places that haunt us.

Retirement time

In the early days of 2003, due to a Revenue Canada determination regarding 'Supplemental Pensions,' I chose to retire from law enforcement after 28 years of service, at the age of fifty-two. Four days later, I began working for a software company that produces laptop tracking software. As a Theft Recovery Officer, my function was to serve as a liaison with various police departments in jurisdictions throughout North America and, to a lesser extent, worldwide. Shortly into my tenure, I was promoted to Operations Manager. I hired several retired VPD members as Theft Recovery Officers, oversaw the ongoing files, and helped to develop creative recovery scenarios resulting in a success rate not previously enjoyed by the company.

Eventually, I was offered the position of Vice President of Recovery Services, a position which would require me to commute to the downtown core five days a week and to be on-call on weekends — not something I was eager to do. I declined the position and helped the company find someone to fill the void. In due time, after the position was filled, I found myself without a contract and that ended my tenure with the company.

As a contractor, I was able to form my own private investigation firm. It was a successful venture, so I continued with it for a short time. Ultimately, though, I didn't find the work rewarding enough to justify the amount of time and expense I was giving to it, and it was then I decided to retire for good this time, having reached the ripe old age of fifty-nine.

In the late summer of 2009, a former colleague alerted me to a position the RCMP was attempting to fill with a retired member, working with the Intel Hub of the Combined Forces Special Enforcement Unit (CFSEU). The unsworn position required a very high security clearance and law enforcement contacts were an ongoing, necessary asset. I called the RCMP NCO heading the unit and he invited me to come in for an interview. Having met the required qualifications, I was hired as a Subject Matter Expertise (SME) analyst within the Intel Hub.

Our primary function was to monitor all police reports submitted in the B.C. Lower Mainland for known gang members and associates; we would then compile a daily intelligence bulletin detailing those movements and activities for dispersal among all Municipal Police Departments and RCMP Detachments in B.C. and Alberta.

As with most things in the policing world, new bosses meant new brooms and constant change is perceived as a necessary element of daily operations. I was moved from the Intel Hub at CFSEU to the Gang Task Force and became a disclosure clerk, redacting materials relating to a high-level murder investigation involving one of the luminaries of the gang world. I stayed with this position for one year, at which point I had finally decided the world of policing would not fall apart if I left, and in March of 2013, I finally retired for good.

Reflecting back over my career, I've witnessed considerable changes to policing, much of it for the better. What has remained unchanged, however, is how the job affects its members. PTSD is a common affliction among officers and it can have devastating implications. I believe now more than ever members must have immediate access to counselling and we must all work toward putting an end to the stigma attached to seeking help.

The Perfect Vision of Hindsight

Hindsight is nearly always perfect vision. While some of my recollections are likely skewed with my perceptual acuity, for the most part I believe my life experiences have not injured me too terribly. Certainly, I do recall a number of events that stood out and fostered some discomfort, but I've always seemed able to get through them relatively unscathed. I can remember shedding tears the night Larry Young was shot and killed during a drug raid. I remember the fear that shot through my heart the night I was stabbed with an AIDS-infected needle by an addict; the six months I had to wait for the 'all clear' seemed a lifetime, and I was sure I was going to contract AIDS and die. I remember being gutted when the young lady jumped off the Burrard Bridge and I remember the endless torment of second guessing my actions. There were so many high-voltage situations that created sadness, fear, anxiety, and panic, but they all eventually faded into the background of life.

The shift work, lack of sleep, court cases and the constant battle to do the job causes a good number of good coppers to experience PTSD, including myself. I am immensely proud of my service and I know I helped people through some horrible times. There have been times I have needed help. I am not afraid or ashamed to admit I have sought help, and will continue to do so when I think it is required. One truly valuable lesson I've come to realize is I can't fix some aspects of my life and I can't change the way other people think or behave; all I can do is concentrate on doing whatever I can to help myself stay healthy. Sometimes that's pretty hard. I have a lifetime of dealing with foolish and evil people who I could never change to my way of thinking. But these days, I am sleeping quite well.

Sharon Bourque is Métis and was born and raised in northern B.C. She is a retired police officer (Edmonton Police Service) now working in education. Sharon's passion has always been working with, supporting and mentoring Indigenous youth. After retiring, Sharon received her Bachelor of Education, Bachelor of Arts in Native Studies and Master of Education degrees at the University of Alberta. She is married to Mike, also a retired police officer. They have a daughter Kendra who is also pursuing a career in policing. Sharon enjoys dance, slo-pitch, basketball, sewing and reading.

5

A FULL-CIRCLE EXPERIENCE

■ ■ ■

Sharon Bourque

Tân si n'tôtem'tik Sharon Bourque *nit'siy'hkâson*. Hello my friends. My name is Sharon Bourque. I am Métis and was born and raised in northern British Columbia. My mother is of Cree and Scottish ancestry and is from Peavine Prairie, Alberta. My father is of Cree and French ancestry and is from Lac La Biche Mission, Alberta (the Mission). I am the older of two girls. My parents separated when I was thirteen years old. Mom moved out of the house leaving dad to raise my sister (eight years old) and me with no immediate family supports. Dad believed that to get ahead in life we needed an education and that meant graduating from high school.

What I remember is that I did not get to experience my teenage years like my other girlfriends, as I went from being a thirteen-year-old girl to becoming a mother to my younger sister. I went to school to learn and also played on the school sport teams, but when I got home my role switched from being a teenager to that of a mother role. I prepared the meals, cleaned the house and did laundry while looking after my younger sister.

I looked forward to summer as Dad would take us girls to the Mission for summer holidays. We swam every day in the lake with our cousins, picked berries with Grannie and went to Church on Sundays. These were happy times where I could just be a kid and not worry about anything.

Yet, as I reflect back on my childhood, we did not live the Métis way of life. My dad, sister and I did not live in a Métis community. The town we lived in was a small farming community and was predominately white. Although Dad acknowledged our Métis heritage, he explained that times were tough for Indigenous Peoples back in the 1970s and he did what he thought was best and that was to have us blend into mainstream society. Today I am a wife, mother, daughter, sister, auntie, friend, advocate, educator, and helper. I am also a retired police officer.

My Own Voice
I started off by telling you who I am and where I come from. It is good to know where you come from as it makes for better relationships with other Indigenous people. It also creates space so that we have something in common — our Indigenous relations. This is something that I learned early on in my career as a police officer and which I carried with me into my second career in education. I speak and write truly from my own experiences and perspectives and do not represent Indigenous Peoples' voice. The only voice I can represent is my own and this is where I place myself.

My journey into policing as a Métis woman came with its fair share of challenges. A story that has always remained particularly vivid in my memory is an investigation early on in my policing career that came full circle into my career in education. For me, this event feels like it happened yesterday.

Before policing, my goal was to become a physical education teacher just like my English teacher/volleyball coach who was my role model and mentor. Instead, a high school career fair completely changed the course of my career plans.

Out of curiosity, I had attended an RCMP information

session. I remember walking into the classroom and seeing all boys — I was the only female in attendance. Needless to say, after the presentation by the male RCMP officer I was hooked, and my goal was, henceforth, to become a police officer.

After graduating from high school, I moved to Edmonton to pursue a career in policing. I began working as a civilian member with Edmonton Police Service because I believed this would be the best setting to gain experience, knowledge, and understanding of the police culture. I worked hard and had a few female police officer friends and role models that I looked up to.

It took me many tries with my police applications to get accepted. I endured a lot of hard work and tears but I believed in myself, persevered, and made it through. I received the good news from my female police officer friend and mentor who was pregnant with her first child and who worked in the recruiting section. Shortly after receiving the news, I met with the recruiting sergeant who congratulated me and shared that they had two concerns about me; they were concerned about how I would do academically, and that I would get fat. I remember this conversation like it was yesterday.

After completing recruit training, I was assigned to South Division Patrol and was partnered to work with the most senior member in the squad. In the police vehicle he said, "You should be at home, barefoot and pregnant." He continued to say that I had two strikes against me, "You are female, and you are Native."

Needless to say, my journey into policing was a tough go from the get start. The hurdles that I had to overcome to prove that I had what it takes was emotionally, mentally, physically, and spiritually draining. I never did fit into the box but I got the job done and I did it well. A constant message that I have told Indigenous youth during my policing career and now in education is, "Be proud of who you are and where you come from. Don't change being who you are so that you can fit into the box."

After working three and a half years in South Division, I transferred to Downtown Division Patrol. The reason? I wanted to work downtown as there were a number of Indigenous People living in the inner city. I had also just started my Native Studies degree at the University of Alberta and I wanted to learn more about Indigenous Peoples and their history and how I could better serve them. I was also on a personal journey to learning more about myself as a Métis woman.

The Crime

In 1991, I investigated an impaired driving case, which involved a stolen vehicle. I was working first watch, just my briefcase and me. It was 0630 hrs. and I was driving eastbound on Princess Elizabeth Avenue in a marked police vehicle approaching Kingsway Mall in Edmonton. I observed a four-door car pull out in front of me. The vehicle was straddling both the number one and number two lanes and was driving under the speed limit. It then drifted over to the curb lane and would speed up then slow down. This pattern continued until we came to the intersection at 106 Street. The vehicle stopped briefly then made a left turn onto 106 Street, northbound while the traffic light was still red.

I notified control that I had a possible impaired driver and requested a stolen vehicle check which came back negative. I then activated my overhead lights to do a vehicle stop; however, the suspect's vehicle continued driving north bound on 106 Street and made a left-hand turn onto 118 Avenue, west bound on a red light, making no attempt to stop for it. The suspect's vehicle then made a right-hand turn, north bound, as it had nowhere else to go and immediately pulled into a vacant parking lot and stopped. I advised control of our location and started to approach the suspect's vehicle on foot when it began driving away from me at a low speed.

I ran back to my vehicle and notified control. The suspect's vehicle made a left-turn, south bound, onto the road and began to drive at a very high rate of speed, which I estimated to be 120 km/hr. It was like a scene out of *The Dukes of Hazzard*. The suspect's vehicle went airborne and hit the light standard head on with such force that the bottom of the light standard — cement and all — came right out of the ground. Time slowed down. The suspect's vehicle landed upside down in a parking lot. When I got out of the police vehicle and approached the suspect's vehicle, I could hear a girl's voice crying, "I want my Mommy."

There were two female occupants in the vehicle. There were broken beer bottles all over the ground. EMS and Fire responded with the jaws of life, along with members of my squad who took over the collision investigation. After the driver was extracted from the vehicle and placed onto the gurney, I followed her and the paramedics to the ambulance where she was placed in the back. Once inside the ambulance I arrested, chartered and cautioned the driver of the vehicle (suspect) for impaired driving and rode with her to the hospital.

Once the suspect was placed in the examining room in the Emergency Department, I continued with my police investigation. I learned from a fellow squad member investigating the collision that he had spoken to the registered owner of the vehicle who confirmed that the vehicle had been stolen. I explained to the attending doctor that I had reasonable and probable grounds to believe that the suspect was impaired by alcohol and because of her physical condition, it would be impracticable for me to obtain a sample of breath from her and that I would like to do a blood sample. The doctor examined the suspect and advised me that he was of the opinion that the suspect was unable to consent to the taking of samples of her blood. I advised the doctor that I would be applying for a telewarrant to obtain a blood sample from the suspect. A telewarrant is a warrant that is requested by telephone to a judge. This was my first and only time doing a telewarrant during my entire policing career.

I provided information to the judge on oath that I had reasonable and probable grounds to believe the suspect had,

---

His Kokum (grandmother) then came to the door.
She looked at me hard,
then shouted to her grandson,
"Oh my God. It's her. She saved your mother."

---

within the preceding four hours a) committed impaired driving as a result of consumption of alcohol, b) the suspect was involved in an accident resulting in bodily injury to themselves and a passenger, and, c) that the attending doctor was of the opinion that the suspect was unable to consent to the taking of blood samples and that taking the blood samples would not endanger the life or health of the suspect

I confirmed that 'Tina' (a pseudonym) the driver of the stolen vehicle was fourteen years old and her female passenger was thirteen years old. After obtaining the telewarrant, I observed blood samples being taken from the suspect by the doctor. The vials of blood were turned over to me. I immediately returned to police headquarters and turned the vials of blood in to the Forensic Identification Section. After completing my investigation, the appropriate charges were laid and the case went to Youth Court. The accused pleaded guilty and was sentenced. In most cases this is where the story would end. But not in this case.

A Surreal Experience
In 2006, I was working as a School Resource Officer at seven inner-city elementary and junior high schools. The Principal at one of the junior high schools asked if I could drop off a suspension letter to a parent, as they did not have a telephone. I went to the address of the fourteen-year-old grade 9 student to deliver the letter. I knocked at the door. The student answered and it was apparent that he was not happy to see me. His Kokum (grandmother) then came to the door at which time I identified myself and stated why I was there. Kokum looked at me hard, then shouted to her grandson, "Oh my God. It's her. She saved your mother." Kokum then called the mother who came out from another room.

The mother was Tina, the driver of my stolen vehicle/impaired driving file from 1991. She told me if it hadn't been for me, she wouldn't be alive today. This was a surreal experience. Something I will never forget. To this day — and it has been thirty years — I can still paint a clear picture of what happened, how time stopped when the vehicle went airborne, hit the light standard head on and then flipped over landing on its roof. Then, how time sped up.

Reconnecting with Tina through her son is an experience I have never forgotten and never will. Was it fate? I don't know. On November 9, 2006 I officially retired from the Edmonton Police Service so that I could continue with my last year of studies at the University of Alberta. My plan was to retire after 25 years police service and to embark on another career in education. In June 2008, I received my combined degrees in Bachelor of Arts in Native Studies and Bachelor of Education. Shortly after, I was hired by Edmonton Public Schools as a teacher and began working in the Aboriginal Education Unit as a teacher consultant.

Coming Full Circle

By 2014, I was working at a local high school as the First Nations, Métis, and Inuit (FNMI) Coordinator/Counsellor. My role was to support the achievement and wellbeing of Indigenous students who self-identified as First Nations, Métis, or Inuit. This also involved visiting local junior high feeder schools and connecting with the grade 9 FNMI students.

My journey has included learning about who I am as an Indigenous person — a Métis woman, in the male-dominated profession of policing

---

During registration at one of the junior high schools I was sitting with a grade 9 male student and reviewing his registration forms. While scanning the form I recognized the name of his legal guardian who was his Kokum. I asked if his mother was Tina. He said, "Yes. How do you know?" Tina's name was not listed on the form. I said here is my business card. Give it to your Kokum. She will know who I am. Later that day, I received a phone call from Kokum and we briefly reconnected. Kokum was, of course, the mother of Tina, the driver (accused) in my impaired driving/stolen vehicle investigation from 1991. Life had not been kind to Tina. She'd lived a hard life and had been killed by her partner in a domestic violence situation. Kokum was now raising the children.

As I reflect, I realize I have come full circle. My journey has included learning about who I am as an Indigenous person — a Métis woman, in the male-dominated profession of policing. I am grateful for the skill set that I acquired during my policing career. These skills have been transferable into my various roles within education since retiring from Edmonton Police Service in 2006.

Because I love to learn, I continued with my education studies at the University of Alberta and completed my Master of Education Degree in Theoretical, Cultural and International Studies in 2013. I have been blessed to work in a variety of roles in education as a teacher, consultant, assistant principal, FNMI Coordinator/Counsellor and now as a Graduation Coach. My passion has always been about making a difference. Being a role model and mentor to Indigenous youth; supporting, mentoring, coaching and advocating for them. Challenging? Yes. Rewarding? Yes. I have no regrets with the career paths I have chosen. Life is what you make it to be.

At sixteen, Neil Masson became a member of the Canadian Armed Forces and spent nine years in the army. As an Engineer he learned how to build bridges and roads and also how to blow them up. In 1968 he joined the Brampton, Ontario police service and was invited to join the Tactical Unit where he used his expertise with explosives. After retirement, Neil became a craftsman and an avid fisherman. He has been married since 1964, and has two children and three grandchildren.

6

A LITTLE GIRL NAMED ROSE

■ ■ ■

Neil Masson

WITHIN THE FIRST NINE YEARS of joining the Peel Regional Police Department, I'd spent two years on the Tactical Team, three years on the Bomb Squad, a year in the Communications Bureau, and a year in the Criminal Investigations Branch. While on the Tactical Unit and Bomb Squad, I did regular patrol shifts but was subject to 'call out' should the need arise. I had made First Class Constable in a little under two years. Because of my grades at police college and a couple of arrests I'd made during Break and Enters, I was given advancement towards reclassification as a reward for good work and initiative. I'd passed my promotional exams and done well on my interview and was just awaiting the list of promotions to be published. Once all of the interviews were complete, the list was posted; I had made Sergeant and transferred to the Brampton Division. It had been just a little over nine years since I left the military, Royal Canadian Engineers, until this promotion.

A Weird Incident
One of my first calls as a sergeant came in the early summer on a sunny Sunday afternoon. I was a brand-new patrol sergeant working the day shift in Brampton when

the radio came on asking for any unit within the vicinity of Lisa Street.

I replied, "Sergeant 21A is close. What is the call?"

They replied, "Sgt. 21A, there is a found child at the apartment building on Lisa Street. See the complainant in 202."

"10-4," I replied, "and you may as well mark me 10-7 because I'm just about there."

Now, a found child is not an unusual call, but the fact it was in an apartment building was a little different. I assumed the child wandered away and someone in the same complex would soon call to report a lost child. But this was to be like no other found child call I had ever done, or ever did, in all my years on the road.

I parked my cruiser and buzzed Unit 202 to be let in. I was met at the door by a young Caucasian couple and the woman was holding a small child about two years old, possibly younger.

The child was Black and clutching the woman for all her might. "I assume this is the child you've found," I asked.

"Yes," she replied.

This is where things got weird. The young woman stated that she and her husband had just returned from shopping and as she was putting the groceries away, she heard a noise on the balcony. She looked in the direction of the noise and there stood a young Black child on her balcony, crying.

The couple lived on the second floor, so there was no way the child could have climbed up or down. The apartment door had been locked as well, and the couple had used their key to get in. Regardless, this child was not tall enough to reach the doorknob. In any event, they knew their neighbours both above and below and neither had a child.

I asked them to call the building superintendent to

see if they knew the child. A few minutes later, the building super arrived and immediately recognized the little girl, "That's Rose, and she lives on the seventeenth floor with her mom and dad." So, together we headed up to the seventeenth floor and knocked on the door of their apartment.

"Who's there?"

I replied it was the police, and after the eyepiece blacked out for a second or two, the door opened to a Black woman in her thirties or early forties.

She immediately exclaimed, "Rose, baby!" Looking at me in shocked confusion, she asked, "Where did you get her?"

I explained the lady with me had come home from shopping and found Rose on their balcony on the second floor — fourteen stories below.

The woman was Rose's aunt and was looking after her while her parents were at church. Rose's father was a pastor at a local church and was delivering the sermon that day. The aunt went on to explain that she had fallen asleep on the couch and Rose must have left the apartment.

The apartment door was locked, but the balcony sliding door was ajar. I went out to the balcony and found a chair had been pushed up against the table, which was tight against the railing. Rose had climbed up onto the table and while looking over the edge had fallen off! Since there is no way anyone can survive a fourteen-story fall, I looked over the edge and saw what had happened: The balconies were in the process of being painted and scaffolding was suspended by cables from the roof; the scaffold was up tight against the balcony on the second floor.

I returned to the second floor unit to look at the scaffolding. It was then I noticed there was a chicken-wire safety net around the outside of the building to prevent tools from dropping on someone below. The wire was compressed in the middle of the scaffold — this is what Rose had landed on, compressing the wire as she dropped into the balcony of Unit 202.

By this time, Rose's parents had come home and were informed about what happened. Rose appeared unhurt, but as a precaution I suggested they take Rose to the hospital and have her checked for injuries. After an examination, she was released with only a few minor bruises. The story was picked up by a tabloid and the father said that angels had carried his daughter down.

I am not a particularly religious person and don't put much stock in miracles, feeling they are mostly coincidence. I often reflect on this call and wonder how that little girl made out. She surely was a miracle child and someone was definitely looking after her that day.

Not Another Statistic
That incident played on my thoughts more than any other of the hundreds of calls I attended over the twenty years I spent on the road. As I approached retirement, I decided I was not going to be another statistic; I was going to spend my retirement doing things with my wife as well as things I always wanted to do.

Going into retirement was not an easy process. Oh, I could play more golf and hockey, but that only took up a small portion of my time. I wanted something that challenged me and gave me satisfaction and hopefully fulfillment and I wanted something removed from policework. The sudden passing of friends before their time and the miracle of little Rose made me realize how fickle life could be. I had always dabbled a little with woodwork, but my skill level and general knowledge was sadly lacking, and I had no idea where to start.

I was quite serious in my desire to become a decent woodworker. I went online and found several woodworking shows that were upcoming and not too far to travel to.

I spoke with several vendors and met one gentleman who gave lessons every Saturday. His shop was close and he still had room so I signed up for the course. He was a master cabinetmaker, which helped immensely.

After attending these classes every Saturday for about a month, I had realized this was what I wanted to do. I purchased some of the basic tools and turned my garage into my own workshop. I started making Muskoka lawn chairs, which I then gave to lucky friends and relatives. I then decided to start a project that would really test my newly found skills: I decided to remake all my kitchen cupboards. This is when I learned the most important rule, and it must be followed, no matter your level of woodcraft: Measure twice and cut once. I learned this rule the hard way, unfortunately more than once.

It took me all winter and well into spring before I had the cupboards completed. After their construction, I still had to stain and varnish them but had no idea how to proceed. Back to my teacher for more instruction. Some of my projects required thirty coats of varnish with light sanding between each coat. It really tests your patience when you're anxious to see the end product. About a month or so later, the job was done and the cupboards proudly hung. I received many compliments and felt very satisfied.

I continued with my woodworking and started making furniture. I have made beds, cabinets, desks, bathroom cabinets, Muskoka chairs, hope chests, and a number of small knick-knacks for friends and family. I had found my niche and it offered me a great deal of satisfaction and fulfillment.

After leaving the force, I also wanted something that taxed my abilities and kept my brain active. Policework had provided that challenge for me on a daily basis, but my future was 'retirement'. I missed the people more than the job; that's pretty much the case for all of my retired friends. Carpentry was nothing like policework but, strangely enough, the process remained the same in that I started each task from scratch with no clear knowledge of what the job entailed or where it would lead. I went to the police academy for my policing job, and carpentry school for my hobby. There was a learning curve in both activities and a sense of pride with the completion of each step. Woodwork was my salvation and kept me from becoming a couch potato.

Apart from carpentry, we purchased a travel trailer and my wife and I tried camping in the southern USA. We camped most years for the month of April. April is a terrible month, by the way — no fishing, no golf, no skiing, and worst of all, no hockey. (I play in an old-timer's league a couple of times a week all year round.) When we got back home in May, we would take our golf clubs, hone our game and get a head start on our handicap.

This changed somewhat when I was introduced to surf fishing. I purchased a Florida saltwater licence and an inexpensive saltwater rig. I must have caught a hundred fish that first year and, pardon the pun, I was hooked.

One memorable fishing story that comes to mind happened while I was surf fishing one morning in Florida. When I checked my rod, I felt a strong resistance. I began to reel in and the resistance became much greater. I thought I had hooked a shark or a ray because I had caught both before and this felt similar.

As I continued to reel in, a crowd formed, all anxious to see the giant fish. People were videotaping me and the crowd grew larger — there must have been thirty people gathered, all offering me encouragement as I wrestled the beast aboard. When I finally reeled my fish in close to shore, there was a collective laugh from my audience. I had just landed a six-foot beach towel! Talk about embarrassing. You can imagine the comments. "How d'you clean that?" "What do they taste like?" "What's the best way to cook 'em?" I just gave them a stupid grin, shrugged, and rebaited my hook.

Picking up and passing along
My sixteen years after the force were both rewarding and fulfilling, but I must say a final word about policing. I receive the Retirees Association Newsletter and it includes all of the current events within the Peel Regional Police. I have seen three of my officers rise to become Deputy Chief of the service, with several more becoming superintendents and many others advancing to staff sergeants and sergeants. I would like to think that in some small way I contributed to their successes and this makes me very proud.

Meeting new people is like walking unprotected through a crime scene. A hair drops from your head or you pick one up on your shoe as you leave — and in doing so, you have just changed the crime scene forever. When you meet someone new, you pass on something of yourself to them and pick up something from them in return. Your meeting has changed both of you, forever. This was what little Rose did for me. From the day I first met her and until the day I die, I will remember that day. It was my most memorable, life-changing experience. I wish I could have followed the life of Rose to see how she used her miracle. I hope she became a doctor, a nurse, a teacher, or any profession geared toward helping others. As with many others I've come across over the course of my career, I guess I will never know.

Before advocating for first responders, Elizabett Cordeiro was once one herself, serving twenty seven years with the Toronto Police Service. Retiring as a detective-sergeant she fondly reflects on her career and her contribution to specialized investigations and frontline operations while cherishing the camaraderie shared with her brothers and sisters in blue. She is known for her love of music, the arts and travel but most notably for the love she carries for her two daughters.

7

THE THIN BLUE LINE

■ ■ ■

Elizabett Cordeiro

One can never tell what goes on behind closed doors, but one wonders. As coppers, we patrol our neighbourhoods not knowing who occupies the homes that line the streets, or which house we'll be called to next. Part of our job is to maintain some level of visibility to our communities and proactively police, where time permits, while being at the ready when a hot shot comes over the air—and there are many.

I started my career as a rookie in a very densely populated part of the inner city with some of the highest calls for service. As busy as it was, there was always a sense of mystery around who we were actually protecting. One night on a midnight shift when things were, dare I say, 'quiet' my partner Jim, who was driving, went out of our zone to an unassuming street and parked. I asked him why we were there and he just grew silent and stared out the window for what seemed like forever saying nothing. When I looked over at him there were tears streaming down his face. He finally pointed out towards one of the houses and said something along the lines of "what happened behind those doors was a type of horror I will never forget … a horror that will forever haunt me." He didn't tell me what happened there on that particular night, but he did go on to share details of the horror as the trust and bond between us as partners grew.

You Can't Lead if You're Not Followed

Before I get into the impacts of that investigation I'll first tell you a little bit about myself. I was born and raised in the city of Toronto so it was quite something for me to end up patrolling the streets I roamed as a kid. My parents emigrated from Portugal over fifty years ago with no aspirations to go back. My father proudly served as an infantry soldier with the Portuguese Army and the stories he shared both inspired and moved me. While you might think those stories were mainly about oppressive and exploitative colonialism they weren't.

My father was ahead of his time when he spoke about his understanding of the African liberation movements and the humanitarian needs that were grossly overlooked. I was overwhelmed with pride when I was in São Miguel, Açores (unfortunately after my father had passed) speaking with a young soldier who proudly reflected on what my fathers' 18th Battalion accomplished despite the difficulties they faced, much of which still informs tactics in use today. My father didn't dwell on the historical impacts of his service and rarely spoke of the risks that came with his bravery. At that time, enlisting was mandatory but my father saw it as an opportunity, as he did most things. He told stories about the strong, compassionate leaders who led him and of the ones who shouldn't have. He would always say to me as I progressed in my own career, "You can't lead if you're not being followed," and those words stuck with me and guided me as a servant leader.

Amidst his pride, strength, and bravery, I knew my dad had seen things he wished he'd never seen. There were times when I would lose him as his mind travelled back, his eyes welling with tears. I'd sit patiently, waiting and wondering if he would ever share what caused them but he always said I didn't need to know the ugly side of humanity and often encouraged me to seek work that would keep me closer to the brighter side. I suppose his encouragement wasn't quite enough. Despite knowing it has its share of darkness, I was pulled towards policing and joined the Toronto Police Service when I was just shy of nineteen years old, fresh out of high school.

After joining the job I came to learn all too well what my dad meant and how it would feel to carry the heaviness of it all. Our roles reversed and I became the one sharing stories, often as tears formed, and he would wait and wonder if I could share what caused the tears. But I couldn't, because we, as coppers, too often simply can't.

I knew he worried about me a lot, as did the rest of my family and friends. There were many times I pulled away from those close to me because of what I was exposed to on the job, but fortunately I always found my way back. When I did, my dad was always ready to sit and talk, or just listen. To lighten things up he'd give me advice on how to "catch bad guys." Would we ever laugh. He was pretty crafty, and back in those days some of his suggestions might have 'flied'! (nothing illegal mind you). And to that point, what I appreciated most was his wisdom around how to be resilient. He would tell me I should stay close to my faith to guide me through the trauma, sadness, and heartbreak — to lean on my faith to help me discern which paths were laid before me and despite how jaded and emotionally and physically exhausted I'd feel at times, to hang onto the belief that sharing the burdens of others is a task that allows us to move through life with purpose, inspiration, and humility.

A Skilled Investigator
Throughout my career I was entrusted to lead countless investigations, specializing in the areas of child abuse, domestic violence, and sex crimes. I also proudly represented the Service as its Child Abuse Coordinator. Most of the cases we, in this line of work, would take on were based

on horrifying, unfathomable acts of violence towards the most vulnerable in society. These unfathomable acts were often committed by persons of trust with exclusive opportunity to harm vulnerable victims — people they often looked up to and felt safe with. The monsters they loved.

Over the years I became a skilled investigator and was asked to take on various roles or projects that, in some cases, I ended up having to respectfully decline.

These unfathomable acts were often committed by persons of trust ... people they often looked up to and felt safe with. The monsters they loved.

I did so because as a mother of two daughters (who at the time were the target age of most of the offenders I encountered) I knew I had to be cognizant of how the work was effecting me and how in turn it would impact my ability to parent. Have I mentioned how fierce I am when it comes to my girls? Everyone who knows me knows they are my absolute everything. I'm grateful I had the awareness and foresight that allowed me to maintain a balance between being a cop and being a mom. It wasn't easy though, especially as a single mom, and at different stages in my career and with increased responsibilities, there were a lot of sacrifices I had to make which took precious time away from them. Truth be told, I could have easily made a career of putting sexual offenders and child abusers in jail, but I am grateful I was able to make the decision not to. I'm even more grateful for my colleagues who dedicated themselves to doing this work. They're a special kind of hero.

While many cases and victims leave a mark in my mind and on my heart, it is the one I'm about to share with you that left the deepest impact on me early on in my career. It is because of how it affected my partner, Jim Vaughan-Evans. Cases like this never leave us.

Jim's Agony
As all rookies are, I was part of a generalist training program that took me off the street for six months and placed me into my first investigative spot in the Youth Bureau. Luckily for me, Jim was already up there and I landed on his team. The mandate of the office was to investigate all youth-related and child abuse-related crimes. I couldn't believe how busy it was and how heart wrenching the work became. I gained knowledge every day and was in awe over the care and attention Jim and the others paid to their work and, in particular, to the victims and their families.

Jim started to open up to me and eventually told me what happened in the house on April 24, 1996 when he experienced the horror that would forever haunt him. He told me an unthinkable story of child abuse and neglect so shocking that it is no wonder that the terror of its memory would awaken him with screams and cries. He would cry over the memory of a six-month-old child named Sara who died because of abuse inflicted on her by her parents Lisa Olson and Mike Podniewicz. Remembering the terrible suffering of Sara's older siblings, who were also abused, also made him weep. He mentioned how lifeless baby Sara's body was when he found her and how images of the scene and signs of neglect and horror kept him awake at night. Pathology revealed that Sara's arms and legs were broken and that ribs were fractured as well. She weighed only ten pounds when she died of untreated pneumonia and her brother Stephen was so badly beaten that he was, and still remains, in a vegetative state. Her sister, Jasmine, a victim of ongoing physical and sexual abuse could do nothing to protect herself or her siblings. She too survived but Jim often wonders how.

Baby Sara's tragic passing was heart-wrenching, and what made it especially difficult was hearing about it all from my otherwise fearless partner who could now no longer control his tears when speaking of this case. When he wasn't crying, he would often get a lost, vacant look as he internally travelled right back to the exact day in April 1996 when he had picked up that case. He confided in me about how the trauma of this case and its proceedings had damaged his relationships with everyone he loved, including his own children.

The abusers in this case, Lisa Olson and Mike Podniewicz should never, ever have had the privilege of being parents. They were both found guilty of Second Degree Murder with no parole — fifteen years for the mother and twenty-five years for the father. It was the first time in Canada that parents had been convicted of murdering a child. While you would think this may have rendered Jim some reprieve, it didn't.

At the time, Jim swore me to secrecy. Back then you suppressed your inability to process or cope with the traumas inherent to the job — it was a time when you were reminded, "This is what you signed up for," or we were told to just, "Suck it up or quit." That was really the extent of the support we were given, so we were forced to stifle impacts of trauma for fear of reprisal, and as if that wasn't bad enough, then came the stigma. The phrase in policing, "We often eat our own" comes to mind.

I listened to Jim's anger about how this child's death was eroding his spirit and faith in humanity, how there was systemic injustice bounded by the inadequacy of protective child services, and how disappointed he was in people who failed to report the danger the children were in. Every day, sometimes completely out of the blue, he would ask, "How could that have happened? How did nobody catch on that they were in danger and needed protection?"

I have asked myself the same question over countless cases I've investigated but my partner's questions were burning him up — they were taking over his thoughts and his ability to cope. It seems he just couldn't erase the images in his mind or let go of the guilt he felt for not saving them from the abuse and neglect that ultimately led to Sara's death and Stephen and Jasmine's own injuries. The combination of all this trauma disrupted Jim's life and ravaged his emotional wellbeing. Every time he brought it up he would understandably cry. I could literally see and feel his heart breaking, and still do when I think of it and when we chat. He told me I was the only person he trusted enough to openly speak with about the weight of his distress. While I was grateful to be in a position to be there for him, it was heartbreaking to know he felt that way. There had to be a better way to deal with this.

Eventually, the burden became too much. He became angered by every case we picked up. Even driving to a scene or having to meet with witnesses became arduous for him, which in turn, made him difficult to work with. He was irritable and would lash out. His usual compassion and ability to connect with people was gone and I missed it. I picked up the slack when needed but it got tiring. Nevertheless, I was patient because I knew where it was all coming from. Don't get me wrong, I'd call him out on certain things but often with hesitation as I was still considered pretty green at the time and back then you had to know your place. But he knew I was right and responded to my nudging. He would teeter between his old self and the version of himself he had become as a result of that case and all the others that followed.

As time went on and calls increased, work became a

serious grind and it seemed every day there was yet another horrible thing done to someone else and in his mind he just couldn't catch a break. His behaviour became more erratic. In the few moments when we did have some downtime he would pipe up and suggest getting some proactive policing done (our code for finding a great place to eat) but then I'd watch him go from enjoying some of the best food in the city to not wanting to eat anything at all. He went from being the guy who made me shine my boots if there was a scuff from a foot chase to letting his own deportment slip. His mood swings became intolerable and as each day passed, he slipped further away. This was a stark contrast from the go-getter who jumped on every call and investigated crimes with skill and precision enviable to most. It always left me thinking about how I might help, not only him or myself but everyone we worked with. All of Jim's changes were the markings of his affliction with what we now know to be Post-Traumatic Stress Disorder (PTSD) and the impacts were causing him to do things completely out of character — things that were considered a massive betrayal to his colleagues and the Service and more importantly to himself and his family. There's no need to get into what all of that actually looked like but I'm sure you can imagine it wasn't good. Sadly, it wasn't and still isn't in many ways, uncommon.

The Walk-it-off Mentality
Albeit informally at the time, I began sourcing out supports and resources that I felt would help Jim process his trauma and grief. I became well versed in the resources our Employee Family Assistance Program had to offer and even became close with members who ran the unit because, as it turned out, I needed their help as well. I'd struggled with an eating disorder as a teenager, which continued on the job for reasons that were deep rooted through family pressures

of helping to raise siblings and maintaining a household at a very young age. My mother was extremely young when she had us so she didn't have the best parenting skills, and my father was away with work a lot of the time. These facts made it hard for me to be available for extra-curricular sports or just hanging out with my friends after school. Despite that, there was generally a lot of love and laughter in my home, it was still hard and I didn't realize exactly how hard until I got some treatment. While seeing Jimmy, as I call him, and so many other friends on the job struggle, it caused me to really look at how vulnerable I might be to the same issues. If I was going to authentically help out I needed to help myself first. Luckily I did but it wasn't easy.

There was a walk-it-off mentality that existed back then and still exists to some extent today. Although things have started to shift in a more positive direction, there's still much work to be done to alleviate the stigma around mental health. With Jim, the effects of therapy ebbed and flowed. Some days I could see he was back and other days he was lost. It felt like even a coordinated search wouldn't find him. Sadly, Jim faced countless days at risk of harming himself and as he has said so many times, was haunted by Sara's death and cases like hers throughout his career.

He still feels those impacts today, just not to the same extent. The difference between then and now is that he no longer faces the darkness and has reached a complete turning point in his life, finding hope in his happy life on the East Coast, enjoying daily visits at the ocean's edge where he reflects and grows. I always love our chats when we visit and he sometimes shares pictures of his beautiful and peaceful home.

Jim's story is one of many I tell about colleagues who have impacted my career and helped shape the kind of police officer I became. It also speaks to the burden countless others carry from the trauma of critical incidents and moral and occupational stress injuries. Mental health stress, such as what Jim suffered, can lead one to make some really unhealthy and flat-out bad decisions that negatively impact life both on and off the job — the kind that ends marriages just as mine had. Yes, I am part of the stats that make up failed cop marriages, but getting into that would take me off course.

It has been said that the average person will experience one or two major traumas. The average police officer will experience hundreds.

Because of his PTSD, Jim eventually left the job as did many other officers for the same reason. Some unfortunately, didn't make it out alive because their emotional pain and loss of hope overtook everything else. To put it into perspective, think about something really traumatic you've been through and how it made you or someone close to you feel. It has been said that the average person will experience one or two major traumas in their lifetime. In comparison, the average police officer with a twenty-year career will experience hundreds of traumatic calls but even officers who are newer to the job are quickly exposed to the experience of traumatic critical incidents. As time goes on, that one call or the accumulative and compounding effects of many calls, can be and have been devastating.

As for Jim, I'm beyond relieved to say he was one of the lucky ones who was able to get the help he needed to regain a level of mental health and wellbeing that has restored his outlook on life. Here is a poem he wrote as he progressed through his spiritual journey:

FREE

I want to be free, free as a bird,
    Free as the word of God.
Preacher man said, "Son, sit right down.
You wear the sins of your past like a thorny crown.
Don't you think it's time to lay them at His feet?
For it's there they'll stay, there they'll keep.
No need for sorrow, no more tears to weep.
Dry your eyes, 'cause you are free."
I want to be free, free as a bird,
    Free as the word of God.
I went to the church one Sunday morning,
I left there with a feeling of warning.
Those people had what I couldn't get.
And in that church, the night before I was met
with a smile and a hug at the door and they
brought me downstairs for a cup of coffee.
I want to be free, free as a bird,
    Free as the word of God.
And in that room, I found God. It was theirs
but they wanted to share it with me.
And now I am free.

To this day, despite the many years we lost touch, I consider Jim to be one of my closest friends. It speaks volumes to what we refer to as the "Thin Blue Line" because there truly is no greater bond in any profession than the one that comes with service to others. It's a bond that doesn't leave you after the force. It's a lifelong membership and I can't tell you how pleased I am to know that my partner is in a much better place today.

Does One Ever Really Leave the Job?

I'm still getting my head around the fact that I left. And that's not a bad thing, it's just when you commit more than half your life to something it's strange when you stop doing it. The only answer I can come up with, and I say this with utmost certainty, is that the job definitely never left me, regardless of how wonderfully my life has changed.

I hate that I'm even in a position to write about that sudden death/child abuse case or that I can remember countless other cases that would horrify any reader. It saddens me to know that every day there are people being victimized and every day there are police officers and first responders across the board who must continue to shoulder the fallout. A reality too often overlooked is that violent, egregious cases change the lives of everyone involved including civilian support staff. And while affected people diligently do their job, some get knocked off course because they're finding it difficult to cope.

Despite all the hype around it, there is little out there within the entertainment industry that captures the true essence of policing and its reverberating impacts.

In addition to PTSD, empathic strain, formerly known as compassion fatigue, is often suffered by members, supporting victims, families and witnesses. Having to deal with all of this on top of everything else they're expected to do is where officers' families and loved ones start to feel the impacts, often with little to no understanding of why or how they can help. It can take an enormous toll.

What most people don't realize is that policing isn't all its portrayed as. Policing for those that do it is not just a profession, it's a vocation; a calling underpinned by passion and purpose. Despite all the hype around it, there is little out there within the entertainment industry that captures the true essence of policing and its reverberating impacts.

Exhausting physically, emotionally, and mentally, policing is often a thankless job and one that doesn't end once you've signed off after shift. So often late at night when we should be sleeping, it is not uncommon to feel a pull away from those we love towards whatever it takes to escape the pain. The trials and trauma inherent to the job aren't glamorous enough to be cinematized but it's those things that mark the depth of sacrifice involved in signing up. Hero status quickly falls when we can't save a life or have to take someone's life in the interest of public safety. There's a sense of failure, inadequacy, and guilt even if the actions are justified, which is incomprehensible to most, inciting societal outrage and distrust while corroding an officer's wellbeing and intrinsic motivation to do the job.

Living up to 'hero' standards is not an easy undertaking. Putting our lives on the line to protect the lives of others often causes us to repress traumas for our own emotional protection. For some it takes its toll and compromises doing what's actually required to save or gain back control of our own lives. This is where a supportive role, particularly in peer support, is so key. Those suffering just need to know that help is out there and all they have to do is find the courage to ask for it.

I have always been relentlessly committed to my calling to help others. Admittedly, the end of my career in policing came sooner than I thought but for someone who was always going to commute the value of her pension, I was in a great position to look at my numbers and let's just say, they added up. The only downside to it was that I felt like I was peaking professionally and really found my footing in day-to-day operations, and as a leader. Nonetheless, making the decision to go early and give myself some much needed time to reconnect with my beautiful daughters (especially during these challenging times) and to decompress from years of hard work has been an absolute blessing. I take with me a profound sense of pride and accomplishment after having dedicated twenty-seven years of my life to serving the city I love, alongside many members that I will forever hold close to my heart.

Boots on the Ground
The past two years post-policing have been extremely transcendent and restorative for me. I took a deep dive into paradigm shifting by focusing on conscious parenting and intuitiveness around the mind and body. I didn't realize how most of my paradigms had been set on traditional approaches that were mostly control based and how shifting them has really laid down a path to achieving self-mastery in a way I've never known before. It wasn't until I had the freedom of time and gained some stillness that clarity around that emerged. I've let go of so many things that really burdened and limited me. We waste a lot of time on things that just don't matter. I could go on about it but I won't here ... maybe in another book.

So with all the free time I was finally enjoying, I vowed to continue to give back through volunteering as a peer supporter and Strategic Planning Manager with Boots on the Ground (BOTG) and as a Director of Peer Support with Toronto Beyond the Blue (TBTB). Both are external peer support organizations that align me perfectly to helping those on the frontlines, and their families in the integration of work, health and resiliency — all things I'm very passionate about.

By way of background, BOTG was founded by a retired Peel Regional Police Service member, Dave McLennan who, simply put, is an absolute gem. His taking on this mission comes as no surprise. Sadly, over the years he too has seen too many of his colleagues suffer from the impacts of doing the job amidst a policing culture often stuck in a "suck it up" mentality. Sound familiar? His commitment has become his own 'after the force' story, successfully establishing BOTG as a charitable organization providing anonymous, confidential and compassionate support to all first responders across the Province of Ontario.

Dave set out to establish a support network to see that, in his words, "No first responder would go without the support they needed." Most often external peer support programs are founded because the internal, structured workplace-support programs are failing to meet the needs and demands of employees. These come by way of insufficient resources, a lack of effective programming, or because of deeper issues like fear of reprisal or 'sanctuary trauma,' which is by definition when someone who suffers a severe stressor next encounters what was expected to be a protective environment and discovers only more trauma.

All employees, but particularly those in positions of high-risk and trauma exposure, need to know they can access supports in an anonymous, confidential, protective, and nurturing way. Unfortunately we're seeing that these people are having to turn to external supports more often than not. BOTG is a critical response to this need within our community.

BOTG is completely run and staffed by active and retired first responders who volunteer their time offering peer support over the phone or in person, 24/7, as needed. As I write this, there are approximately 160 volunteers who have been trained and over six hundred calls have been taken over the past two years. I've taken several of them myself. There's something wonderful in knowing that when someone doesn't have anywhere else to turn, we can be there to listen. If we have to, we will actively mobilize to assist in person or help with setting up the proper supports and resources to help with addiction, crisis, or mental health. The vision for something like this is one thing but to actually make it happen and to have it impact so many is truly incredible. We owe Dave McLennan a great debt for his vision and efforts and to everyone who has helped him build and sustain them.

All who are involved have an unwavering commitment surrounding mental health by helping officers and their families get healthy and stay healthy.

Beyond the Blue
Where I've dedicated another chunk of my time is with Toronto Beyond the Blue. Like Boots on the Ground, TBTB is another charitable organization very dear to my heart as it supports Toronto Police Service members and their families. It was founded in 2017, sadly, after one of our brothers in blue, PC Darius Garda, tragically took his life after battling years of mental health issues resulting from an on-the-job shooting, leaving his family and his police family devastated and heartbroken.

PC Garda's sister, Dilnaz (Del) Garda recognized the challenges her brother faced both personally and systemically and has since become a strong voice of advocacy for change, building a Toronto chapter and then moving on to lead chapters across our nation as president of Canada Beyond the Blue.

All who are involved have an unwavering commitment to normalizing conversations surrounding mental health by helping officers and their families get healthy and stay healthy. The educational programming, training and practical tools that members receive at no cost to them because of donated dollars helps to equip them and their families with what they need to face whatever challenges life presents, whether it be job related or personal. To date, TBTB has connected over three hundred families.

When I was asked to join the TBTB team, I was both honoured and humbled and am continually inspired by the commitment and compassion of this organization. We operate on a community-based, clinical mental health service delivery model made up of police-informed psychologists and psychotherapists who provide professional guidance towards personal wellbeing, specializing in the treatment of occupational trauma, suicide prevention, grief, loss and resiliency, and post-traumatic growth.

This team is complemented by volunteer peer supporters made up of family members and active and retired members who connect with those in need either over the phone, in person, online, or through group sessions. Through effective marketing, a strong social media presence, a brand ambassador program, peer support services, and awareness initiatives, TPS members and their families know they can reach out to us 24/7, and because they do, we're expanding the peer support team to respond to those ongoing needs and demands.

It's noteworthy to mention that peer supporters, through their shared experience, are well equipped to support others but it's essential that they understand their role is to be a helper not a fixer. This brings to mind the saying: "You may not be able to make things better, but you can make a difference." Each time I hear how we've helped someone find the hope they thought was lost, it reinforces TBTB's motto that, "In our family, no one fights alone."

Sadly, we've lost far too many police members across

our nation to death by suicide and far too many are struggling with mental health and addiction. Suffice to say, it is vital to support those suffering and to normalize and de-stigmatize the effects of trauma so we don't lose anyone else. Organizations such as Boots on the Ground and Toronto Beyond the Blue are certainly doing their part in helping and again, I'm honoured to be a part of this movement.

Despite all the hype around it, there is little out there within the entertainment industry that captures the true essence of policing and its reverberating impacts.

Falls, Losses, Climbs, and Saves — Forever Proud
I'm much better at understanding the effects of trauma at this stage in my life, like most things that came with experience. I was very young when I joined the force and had a lot to learn about everything, including myself, and how to deal with life's falls and losses. But I'm happy to say there were more climbs and saves, both personally and professionally.

Throughout my career, and even now, my family, friends, and many law enforcement colleagues have been there for me and because they have I'm just paying it forward. I wouldn't be standing as firmly as I do today if it had not been for my experience as a police officer and the people I met along the way. And while there's so much about it that I miss, I understand that today's policing landscape is tougher than it's ever been.

If it wasn't difficult enough to take an oath to put

service before self, when we throw in a pandemic, anti-police rhetoric, and uncertain financial resources, support systems become more necessary than ever. The need to emerge triumphantly beyond these times will take resolute commitment by those in the trenches, their leaders, and everyone called to help the helpers. As I navigate my way through this next chapter in life, despite whatever new opportunities may come up, I will always make the time to stand alongside the many who dedicate themselves to helping others and will pray every day for their safety and wellbeing.

Forever proud.

Jimmy's Nightmare
A Response

Jim Vaughn-Evans

■ ■ ■

MEMORY. It's tricky, this memory thing. When I was trying and trying and trying to get well, I never thought about it.

But in order to get well I experienced well-meaning doctors who tried to figure me out. In that effort I was exposed to *so many* prescription medications. So many because none seemed to alleviate my pain. I endured three series of ECT treatments — shock therapy.

I spent weeks at a time in the mental health unit at Oshawa General Hospital. All of that took its toll on my memory.

Those times were extraordinarily upsetting.

So much so that many of my current nightmares relate to my treatment and being well, as opposed to what I saw and experienced at work.

A couple of years ago, while on vacation with my brother, he recounted a memory that he had of us up on the CN Tower. We were on the upper level, where you can go outside. It's clear that it happened but I have zero recall of that moment.

During the same vacation a childhood friend recalled a time when we were at a mutual friend's cottage with a group of our friends. Again, I had no idea what he was talking about.

Conversely, some memories persist.

Telling the sister of Sara that she couldn't see her mother, who was arrested for killing her baby sister, and the pain and tears she had when I told her of the death never go away. Neither does attending the autopsy of Shanay Johnson. I volunteered to attend so I could better do my job at identifying abuse. She suffered abuse on her entire body from the tips of her toes to the top of her head.

There are cases I worked where I know the memories are gone.

Perhaps to protect me.

That doesn't negate their reality, but is rather a symptom of my medical treatments.

There are many intricate symptoms of PTSD. Unique to each sufferer.

It may sound crazy, but I'm grateful for it all. All of it. I wouldn't wish it on my worst enemy because I survived. Many, many, many, *many* others are gone. Leaving loved ones to find answers they will never find.

I'm grateful mostly because through it all I realized my faith. The faith of my parents. The faith of my grandmother. The faith of others that never ever gave up on me. It is without a doubt the cornerstone of my so-called recovery

That's the best I can do 408 (my badge).

I hope it helps.

Just One Person.

1407 (his badge).

JoAnn McCartney is a retired Edmonton Police Service Detective who has been helping sexually exploited women for the past 33 years. While policing and after retiring, she supported women engaging in prostitution to make changes in their lives while successfully bringing their abusers to justice. Since retiring, JoAnn helped create two successful restorative justice programs, and created and facilitated a prison workshop focused on motivating at-risk and already-exploited women to consider change. She has a Master's Degree in Counselling and maintains a private practice working mainly with abused women who have been sexually exploited.

8

MAKING "THOSE WOMEN" STOP
THE TRUTH BEHIND PROSTITUTION

■■■

JoAnn McCartney

Proviso: Throughout this chapter I use the terms prostitute, pimp, and john because I believe in using terms that reflect the harsh reality of this subculture. I do not like terms like 'sex trade worker', 'sex trade consumer' or 'sex trade employer' because they soften the truth of what I have seen. 'Sex trade industry' sounds like some kind of viable business; 'sex work' sounds like a viable type of career. In all my experience, it is not. It is abuse, violence, and exploitation. It is unhealthy people using other unhealthy people to address needs in an unhealthy way.

IT ALL STARTED one day in December of 1987. I had been a Constable with the Edmonton Police Service for twelve years. That day, I was called to the office of the Chief of Police so he could promote me to the rank of Detective. In congratulating me on my promotion, the Chief said he had something to do to me, not with me or for me. He added he was moving someone out to make a spot for me in Morality Control Unit (later called Vice Unit) and then assigned me to "get to know the women out there on the street" to find out "why they were doing what they were doing" and to "make them stop."

There had never been a woman in the Unit with that assignment before and the Chief believed he was being progressive when he put me there. The prevailing attitude of the male-dominated police force was that women prostituted themselves because they were sex maniacs who ruined marriages by seducing men who just happened to be

They taught me that if you look over the shoulder of a prostitute on a corner, you will see a man, the pimp, standing in the shadows watching over her.

driving by. My male colleagues did not buy into the notion that demand (the men) dictates supply (exploited women) even though every other business transaction on the planet works that way. The Chief thought a police woman might be able to connect better with the prostitutes and be able to convince them to stop. The assignment I was given to "make them stop" changed the course of my life.

Woman on the Job
The first few months of my new job were not easy. The Staff Sergeant retired in protest after being forced to have a woman, any woman, in his unit. One of the detectives offered to work with me and teach me the ropes as long as I promised that he would be the first in the unit to have sex with me. Since I had no intention of having sex with any of them, the promise was made. I wanted to learn. I came from life experience that said if you work really hard, you will be accepted. I hoped that this would apply to being a detective because it had worked in other areas of policing where I had

been assigned. It was hard fitting in when a woman wasn't wanted and a popular male had been transferred out to make room for me.

Finally after a year, I found a male detective in the unit who also just wanted to do the work. We started talking to women on the streets, getting to know their stories and trying to convince them to tell us about their pimps and abusers. It was those women who taught me about their lives, their experiences, and their belief systems. At first, I was incredulous that women could be so brainwashed to 'allow' the abuse that was happening to them. But getting to know their stories and seeing them struggle, suffer, and cope, I came to respect their strength and their will to survive. I saw young women get out of a john's car defeated, get in my police car to tell me of the sexual assault she had just suffered and have a good cry. Then seeing her pimp drive past, she would fix her makeup and walk back to her spot on the corner —transforming as she walked from a hurting young girl to an on-the-job prostitute.

These were the young women who taught me how to work undercover as a prostitute so we could arrest johns, the demand side of the problem. They taught me how to stand and walk in five-inch heels — they even knew how to run for their lives in those heels. They taught me how to dress and how to behave with prospective johns to distract them from watching out for clues that I might be a police officer. I became adept at using makeup to create massive bruises on my neck to catch the john's attention and keep him from studying my straight teeth and clear skin. Most importantly, they taught me that if you look over the shoulder of a prostitute on a corner, you will see a man, the pimp, standing in the shadows watching over her. Deal with him they said, and she may just make the choice to try to change. I learned this lesson well and was successful at convicting over a hundred pimps for procuring, extorting, and assaulting women.

Convicting a pimp means supporting the prostituted victim to feel strong enough to stand up in a court and admit to the world what the pimp had done to her even when she had been brainwashed to believe that everything she was doing was her choice. This act of testifying took courage because if she testified, she knew her life and liberty would always be in danger from every other pimp. She would need to leave that world behind and worry for her safety, perhaps forever. Some of the women who turned in their pimps would go on to lead normal lives with normal stressors, but some did not get the long term help they needed to rebuild their self-esteem and trust. Instead, they sank into addiction to numb their pain and shame.

Who are these women I was assigned to stop? Research shows that the vast majority of women who end up being sexually exploited through prostitution were sexually and/or physically abused and neglected as children. Most of them suffer from PTSD, inadequate parenting, inadequate education, and critically low self-esteem before they even begin prostituting. They experience poverty, violence, shame, disassociation, anxiety and other mental health issues and find solace in self-harming coping skills including drug and alcohol use and seeking out abusive men who reaffirm their low value and trauma.

Most of the women I met over the years had pimps at some point who abused and sold them. In the subculture that is prostitution, the pimp makes all the rules and has the right to do anything he wishes to the prostitute, because she is chattel. One of the first young women I met had a baby fathered by her pimp but refused to keep that baby away from him, even when he was violent with her and dangerous to the child. She insisted that because he allowed her to carry the baby to term, she could not prevent him from having it. She said that he beat her often during the pregnancy but because he did not cause her to miscarry, the baby was his to be with as he chose. When he was eventually deported for drug dealing, she was very angry at me for pursuing his deportation because it meant she was being forced to go live in St Lucia to be with her baby there. The baby was, after all, his property. She felt forced to follow him so that she did not lose her baby altogether. I was aghast the first time I heard about this belief system, but I heard it often over the years, and it is a cultural norm that typifies the dominance these men display over the women they own.

Training in Counselling
I worked in Morality Control and then Vice Unit from December 1987 until May 1993 and again from the fall of 1997 until I retired late in 2002. Right after retiring, I went back to school to obtain a Masters Degree in Counselling. All those years of talking to abuse victims and getting them to stand tall against abusers in court convinced me that I could help a lot as a counsellor. I wanted the technical knowledge to be able to help these women in more ways than just trying to talk them into changing their lives.

I believe I have an understanding that few others have of women who have been sexually exploited through prostitution. I have actually walked in their shoes, working undercover, so I know how johns and people generally treat them, and how it feels to be treated that way. I too have stood on a corner and had 'normal' people drive by and throw things like pennies or beer bottles at me, calling me whore or worse. I used to train younger police women to act as decoys to charge johns as well. They would stand on a corner, and if three or four cars passed without a john approaching them, they would start to question themselves. These were healthy, educated women just starting huge careers in law enforcement. I could imagine how a young neglected, coerced or abused woman could have her last vestiges of self-esteem crushed simply by being bypassed by a john.

In school I learned about the psychological consequences of abuse, neglect and exploitation and how to grow beyond that. I understood how their world worked. I had seen enough through policing that no matter what story a woman told me, she did not have to suffer the indignity of seeing her counsellor shocked. Many of the women who saw me for therapy talked of needing to look after previous counsellors because their story was so traumatic that counsellors could not bear to hear it all. Their stories affected me too, but I never reacted with a line like "Oh my God, how did you let that keep happening!?" Instead, I would congratulate them on their strength and will to survive. I understood that their world was much different than the mainstream. I often thought that some of the work we did together could have been labelled cross-cultural counselling because like an immigrant in a new country not knowing the norms, these women did not know how to function in any milieu except the one they were stuck in. They had experienced mainstream culture in the past, and it had been unkind to them, teaching them lessons about their worth that made them vulnerable to the indoctrination of pimps and the street world. To move on, they didn't just need to learn new coping skills, they needed to learn new ways to feel accepted and worthy and wanted in the mainstream world.

My Own Background
Like the women from the street, I grew up in a home I perceived as neglectful, with lots of grief and trauma and poor parenting practices. I spent my teens looking for someone to love me unconditionally and often trusted people I shouldn't have. I had low self-esteem and craved acceptance and attention just as they did. It had become clear to me talking to these women that if I had grown up in a big city instead of small-town Alberta and had been exposed to the

same kind of exploitative men that these women met as young teens, I might have walked a path similar to theirs. Luckily for me, rural life did not pose as much threat as city life. I always made it clear to them why I understood their path and this understanding connected us.

Since retiring and even during my Masters program, I worked in a counselling capacity in private practice, mostly with women who were considering leaving prostitution. I helped create a court diversion program for sexually exploited women who had been charged criminally with minor offences. I helped them execute a plan for change and then vouched for them in court so that their charges could be withdrawn as a reward for their successes. I have counselled both women and men through our local drug treatment court which I also helped create.

The work with male participants in the drug court taught me an understanding of a man's perception of trauma. This helped give me balance because many of the men I worked with suffered from the same sorts of trauma as did the women. I learned that sexual exploitation was about more than men willfully abusing women. Men and boys can also suffer sexual and physical abuse and often learn survival habits that are unhealthy or illegal. I learned to see addiction as a symptom of deeper trauma. I am continually amazed at how unhealed trauma can affect us all.

While still in my Masters program, in an effort to reach more women who were at risk of being exploited, I created and facilitated an empowerment workshop for incarcerated women called 'I Can'. When better to talk to women who could be exploited than when they are sober and fed and have nothing else to do with their day but listen, and perhaps learn?

I presented 'I Can' workshop sessions at two correctional facilities from 2003 until 2020, at which time funding for the program ended. Over a thousand women completed 'I Can' and many more took parts or all of it several times. In that program we talked about how people get dragged into the prostitution milieu, how they cope with it and how to get out. We discussed how abuse and neglect teach a child lessons about themselves and their lack of value, how when a molester says, "You turn me on" it doesn't mean it is the child's fault. We talked about how negative assumptions such as 'I got what I deserved' help create the need for addictive substances and behaviours.

Women coming into the prison would look for my program, and take it over and over because they said it gave them hope that there might be a life after abuse and addiction. Women who I'd had foot chases with as a police officer when they were 14 years old were now 35, in jail, and wanting out the other end of their crime/abuse/ addiction/ exploitation life — and I was still there to help them find a new way to survive. Being a woman and having my experiences meant that I rarely encountered barriers between us — they could be honest with me and I could help them see how normal they were, given their abnormal circumstances in life. To me, their addiction was just their quickest, easiest way to numb out their experiences. Helping with addiction, victimization, and shame was the way to free them and let them create a new future.

I met thousands of exploited women in the last thirty-three years, most of them surviving through some version of selling or trading sex. They were mostly young — the average age of entry into prostitution for a girl in North America is between fourteen and fifteen years old. The average age of exiting that world, in Edmonton at least, was mid-thirties. They were so obviously brainwashed by their 'boyfriends' and believed that their life was what they deserved. One woman told me about growing up with sexual abuse rampant in her family, and about her father who had told her from young childhood that she would never go hungry if she used her vagina to survive.

These women were exploited by their johns and abused by their pimps — whippings and body cavity searches to prevent withholding earnings. If they complained they had been raped by a customer, the pimp would rape them again to teach them what rape really is. Pimps got them pregnant then refused to allow them contact with their babies unless they were absolutely obedient. If they tried to leave, they, their children and their families were either threatened or actually hurt. Some pimps even practiced female genital mutilation — removing a woman's clitoris. It is done so that she cannot enjoy her sex work. I knew of pimps who inserted a hot curling iron into the vagina of a woman who wanted to leave them. This way the woman could not earn money for some other pimp.

These women had nothing. In talking to them over and over however, I found that they actually responded to someone who cared enough to look at their face, to remember their name, who cared enough to not want anything from them except for them to be okay. These women just wanted to feel happy, to feel loved. But because of the abuse and trauma, they didn't even know what happiness or love was. They had learned that their only value was in their ability to provide a sexual service. I believe that my connection with them taught them a little bit about their value. I was someone in authority — a police officer and then a counsellor — and I could still care about them. That told them that they were capable of being cared about by someone who, in their mind, mattered. The women told me their stories, talked of their childhoods, opened up about their fears. Some who had kids taught me of a fierce love for those kids that influenced how I raised my own son. They loved their children, but had no experience of good parenting to help them become good parents so they often repeated the neglect that was normal to them. I met some of their mothers, who taught me about loving your child no matter how bad their behavior can be. I sat with these women in the hospital when they had babies or when they were assaulted and needed medical help. I went to their weddings when they escaped the street and found someone real. Way too often, I went to their funerals when the john or pimp or drug took them by force.

Amanda's Story
One woman, whom I will call Amanda, has been in touch with me for thirty years. I met her in 1990 when she was fifteen and very pregnant. She was at a safe house, and had been assaulted by her pimp. I will never forget how Amanda showed me her pregnant belly and the bruise on her side — you could read the logo 'Levi's' in the bruise where the pimp had beaten her with his belt. I arrested that pimp, but he got bail and moved her to the US where he got her a late-stage abortion. When it came time for court and her testimony, she was unable to cross the border back to Canada to testify. She had no ID proving her citizenship or identity, and as much as I argued with the Border Security guards, they refused her entry into Canada and the pimp's charges were withdrawn. Amanda stayed in prostitution for years — she experienced all sorts of violence including one of her friends being murdered in front of her when they were on a double 'date.' She used mostly alcohol and valium to cope. Her first son, who has Fetal Alcohol Syndrome, was raised by her mother.

Eventually Amanda had another son and decided to clean up and be a mom to him. She heard I had started counselling, so she reached out and I began seeing her professionally. Although she has not officially been in counselling for fifteen years, I still talk to Amanda regularly. Her sons are both grown, are working and in her life. She suffers with health issues like diabetes and hypertension and has survived cancer, but only focuses on giving her sons everything she can. In her forty-five years, her spirit has carried her through all sorts of hardships, but she refuses to submit. This is the kind of strength and perseverance that I saw over and over in the women whom I met and had the privilege of walking beside.

Amy's Story
One of the greatest gifts I have ever been given happened a couple years after I retired. I was contacted by the supervisor of Vice Unit who asked me to email a woman I will call Amy, who had been harassing the unit for my contact information. This woman apparently needed to talk to me directly, not to a Vice cop or any other police officer. I emailed her in Victoria B.C., and as it happened, I was travelling there for a conference a few weeks later so arranged to meet her for coffee. She was a woman I had no particular memory of other than her unusual name.

When I saw her, she told me that she had first met me when she was forced into prostitution by a boyfriend whom she had no idea was a pimp. He had brought her out to Edmonton from British Columbia for a vacation with another couple. When they arrived in Edmonton, his true purpose was revealed. The other couple were a pimp/prostitute combination and she was forced into going to 'work' with this other woman. She was far from home and knew no one to help her in Edmonton, so she complied. She told me that the first johns were terrible, and that she was considering jumping in front of cars so she could be hurt or killed and thus avoid the situation.

Fortunately for her, I came along and checked her as a new girl on the street. She reminded me that I had convinced her to leave her pimp boyfriend, then helped her call a relative in Calgary, got her to the bus, and even paid for her bus ticket. I had no memory of this, but it was something my partner and I did often with women wanting to escape.

The young woman was crying as she told me her story, and I was confused. Then she gave me her gift. She told me she wanted to die that night, intended to die, but I saved her. She had gone on to graduate from UBC as a Special Ed Teacher. She said that her mother had recently died without ever knowing what really motivated her, so she had to find me because she needed me to know that it was all because of what I had done for her. I was dumbfounded, and we both had a good cry together. One just never knows when one does something seemingly inconsequential that changes the life of someone else for the better.

Carved on a Wall
I know that I reached a lot of women like Amanda and Amy, touching their lives, giving them hope and letting them know they are not alone. My phone number has not changed since I first got a cellphone in 1993. I have heard that my number was carved into the wall above the phone on the women's unit at our remand center so that anyone needing advice, a verbal hug or some hope could call. I still get calls from women whom I got to know over the years — they reach out to tell me that they are okay, or that they are not, or that they need to know where to get help. They trust me, and I honor that trust.

Friends of mine wonder why I continue to work; why I still take calls from women who reach out. My response is how could I not? How could I not take a few minutes from my day to let someone who is lonely and hurting know that someone cares enough about them to answer a phone call. It is easy to listen and encourage. It is easy to give advice when asked for it. And I never know when the simple act of my remembering who they are or acknowledging their pain can be the one thing they need to move forward.

My life has been greatly enriched by the connection I

have with the women I have met, by the purpose it has given me. I cannot imagine how I might stop taking calls, or meeting someone for a coffee, or just letting them know that they are someone who is important enough to remember. We all need that. Through all of this, I have learned about the human capacity to be inhuman to other humans. If I can be a tiny bit of something different, I will fiercely be that.

Ernie Louttit was born in Northern Ontario. He is a member of the Missanabie Cree First Nation, raised in a small hamlet called Oba on the CNR mainline. He joined the Canadian Armed Forces in 1978 at 17 years of age. Ernie served with the Princess Patricia's Light Infantry and the Military Police until joining the Saskatoon Police Service in 1987. Ernie Louttit retired in 2013.

9

"THERE IS NO LAW AGAINST IT, CONSTABLE"

■■■

Ernie Louttit

1989 SASKATOON, SASKATCHEWAN

"SNIFFERS" IS HOW SOME POLICE OFFICERS referred to people who abused solvents by inhaling them. Lacquer thinner was the inhalant of choice. It was a shocking and eye-opening form of addiction for me to witness. There was a subculture of about 150 people, if not more, who sniffed lacquer thinner in Saskatoon. Most were youths. Some were as young as ten years old, and almost all were Indigenous. I started dealing with them early in my career, mostly while responding to other crimes. They would be glassy-eyed and sometimes speechless, or at best mumbling, in answering my questions. Often their noses would be running, their balance and reactions out of sync, and they would fight to keep their 'soak' — the piece of cotton or whatever material they had poured the lacquer thinner on — when you tried to take it away from them. The smell was so overpowering it was impossible not to be affected by it when you were dealing with them. Sniffing was the most destructive self-abuse I had seen at that point, until in the later years of my career when meth came along.

At first, I just watched other senior officers deal with them because I had never seen this addiction before and I was still new, which in policing, was the natural order of things. It became more personal once I was out on my own after field training. I was patrolling my area and was by a notorious apartment building where a lot of violent calls originated. All of a sudden this older-model car literally flew out from behind a blind corner and crashed into the passenger side of my patrol car. I looked over and could not see the driver. I exited my patrol car and ran to the driver's side of the vehicle; it was still closed. Crumpled on the floor was a small boy. I pulled the door open and shut the vehicle off. I was immediately hit by the strong odor of lacquer thinner. I got the boy by the arm and pulled him out. I recognized him as the nephew of one of the adult male sniffers. He was glassy-eyed but came around quickly in the fresh air. He told me he was sorry because he couldn't reach the brakes once he got the vehicle in motion.

I called for the Sergeant to come and document the accident. Then I put the kid in the back seat of my patrol car. I established he was only eleven so I knew I could not charge him. At best, I would turn him over to Social Services because, based on my previous experiences with his family, the solvent addiction was multi-generational and I suspected no one would be able to take him in. The car was stolen and was towed from the scene after the Sergeant wrote his report. While waiting for all of this to take place, I had been questioning this kid. "How does the sniff make you feel?" "How long did the high last?" "Where did you get it from?" He was straightforward for my first few questions, but refused to say where he had gotten it.

I had found a small glass juice container with a couple of ounces of lacquer thinner in it on the floor of the car where I had taken him from. I would not know the significance of it until later.

When the two social workers came to the station to retrieve him, they were matter-of-fact and businesslike, giving me the impression this happened all the time. They knew him and he knew them. The drug dealers, pimps, wife beaters, and robbers I could deal with. An eleven-year-old boy stealing cars while high on lacquer thinner was to me just one symptom of a much bigger problem. To be brutally honest, it felt like no one really gave a damn about solvent abuse. The abusers were mostly young First Nations kids — some, but not all, from broken homes and the children of parents with their own problems.

No Law Against It
I spoke with several detectives to see if I could get some direction or tap into what they were doing. It quickly became apparent they had little interest in what they said was basically a "patrol problem" and that they had more important matters to attend to. I went to my inspector and told him about my last call and asked what he thought could be done.

He replied, "There is no law against it, Constable. Just arrest them when you can."

The flippant and dismissive comments from the detectives and my Inspector when I asked about our police service's policy on dealing with inhalant solvent abuse was the motivation for starting an investigation which cemented my policing style for the rest of my career.

In the interest of fairness to some of the senior members of the Saskatoon Police Service in the late eighties and early nineties, these officers had been policing a city which consistently had the highest crime rate per capita in Canada for years. Other than the training they had received on the job, most had minimal or no further training. Post-incident stress and its long-term effects were seen as weakness and were never talked about. Were there some racist attitudes among some of the members? Almost certainly. I just tried to work through or around those individuals.

In 1987, when I started with the Saskatoon Police Service, the population of Saskatoon was about 205,000 people with about ten percent being Indigenous. Indians, Natives, Aboriginal, First Nations; all terms used to identify them — and me — were still very much a part of the everyday language at the time. I had come directly out of the military after almost eight years and everyone to me was just a civilian, even my own People.

I tried not to judge anyone or put much thought into other people's circumstances. I did not really know about Saskatoon or the people. After my first few years, I had definitely swung into believing the people struggling against poverty and constantly being exploited were the people worthy of my best efforts. A hundred and fifty to 200 solvent addicts in a city of 205,000 people does not sound like a crisis, but when the core of them come from a couple of neighbourhoods, the people there see it as one.

I started interviewing every person I dealt with who was high on lacquer thinner, usually after they were arrested for something else. Sometimes there were as many as fifteen people at a sniffing party, which often took place in abandoned houses or low-rent rundown apartments. Almost all the contacts were during night shifts; I believe because of the stigma attached to sniffing solvents. Adults were usually un-cooperative and quite often combative. They had amazingly high pain thresholds and often had to be overpowered.

The amazing thing with both the adults and the youths was how quickly they came down from their highs. In twenty minutes, they could go from glazed-eyed, non-verbal fighters doing whatever they could to keep sniffing or getting away, back to their normal selves. For some of the adult offenders, they just went back to the same unlikeable criminals they were. The youths, both male and female, became teenagers again; some with a weak bravado which quickly left them when you started asking questions which were not meant to trick them or charge them with new offences. They were, for the most part, honest and forthcoming with their answers.

I remember most of them by name. These are just three of the many kids this ultimately involved:

Quentin, a thin, 15-year-old boy who looked like a straight-A-student with his thick-framed, government-issued, 'Indian Affairs' glasses and a shy smile, had no explanation as to why he was sniffing lacquer. He was, however, one of the first to accidentally say where he and the other youths were getting their solvent supply by mentioning an address and then immediately clamming up.

Shelley, a 14-year-old girl from a troubled family, who dabbled in everything and was ruthlessly exploited by many men in her life, sniffed to block it out and hated it. She confirmed the address and gave me a name.

Kelly, a 15-year-old boy who came from a loving family and did not know why he started sniffing, confirmed what the other kids were telling me.

What emerged from these interviews was that the sniffers tended to group together, usually based on their age and social circles. Most, but not all, were sniffing to escape difficult circumstances. Some did it through peer pressure and almost all of them hated it. They were looked down upon by everyone, even criminals, alcoholics and IV addicts. Three adult males were identified as being the main sources providing the lacquer thinner. All of them lived in the neighbourhoods these kids lived in.

Taking flak

I was getting some flak for spending so much time on something that was not even considered a crime. It came from my supervisors and even some of the other patrol officers because they had to take some of the calls in my area when I was tied up. I recorded some of the kids I interviewed using a VHS camera, which was new technology to me and usually the exclusive equipment of the detectives. Night shifts allowed me access because there wasn't anyone around to say differently.

Toluene, when mixed with acetone, affected the white brain matter of abusers; the running noses of solvent abusers was actually brain matter leaking out.

A local reporter came out with me on a night shift to do a story on solvent abuse and did an excellent job of trying to bring the extent of the problem to the awareness of the general population of Saskatoon. She interviewed an emergency room doctor who treated a lot of the chronic abusers who came in high with injuries. He explained the active addictive ingredient was toluene, an aromatic hydrocarbon which produces a euphoric effect when sniffed. It also, when mixed with acetone, affected the white brain matter of abusers; the running noses of solvent abusers was actually brain matter leaking out. The story ran, and in the days before the internet, it was basically one and done. I never received any feedback from the senior administration; good or bad.

To start, I decided to focus on the individual who had been identified the most often. He was a thirty-eight-year-old man. A big guy, six feet tall, weighing around 240 pounds. He often wore his hair in braids which highlighted his scarred face and small eyes. Other times, he wore a

'Billy Jack' cowboy hat. My suspect had a criminal record which was all over the map: assaults, theft, fraud, and driving offences for which he had never done any serious time. He had a big old North American car and lived in a large second-storey apartment pretty much central to my patrol area.

My interviews with the kids revealed my suspect was their main supplier of lacquer thinner. He would drive to different supply stores and buy large cans of it. He would then break it down into small glass juice jars and sell them for five dollars each. Sometimes he would take stolen medications or property in trade, and I suspected, sexual favours as well. He let kids 'camp out' at his apartment. Getting this information was like pulling teeth because a lot of these young people were dependent on him for their 'sniff' and had a sense of loyalty to him because of their addiction. I still did not have enough to charge him with anything. Getting the information was one thing; getting these kids to commit to anything prosecutable was a challenge.

Remembering the conversations with the detectives, the Inspector and the non-response to the television story, I felt I was on my own with this one. The parents of several of the young people were beside themselves, wanting to know what could be done about my suspect because, as almost always, people in the community knew more about him than the police did at the time. They were afraid of him and his extended family. In First Nations communities, there is a connectivity between their home communities and the people in the cities. The extent of it and how it factored into police investigations was just starting to dawn on me. The general mistrust of the police among some Indigenous people in 1989 did not help either.

I was still doing all the other patrol duties during all of this; the call load was always high. Domestic situations, robberies, sexual violence, shoplifting and break and enters were constant sidebars keeping me, I felt, from my suspect whom I had now become laser-focused on.

Off duty, I took to reading *The Criminal Code of Canada*, looking for something that fit. The most obvious section initially was 'administering a noxious substance,' but it did not quite fit because that basically addressed an offence like using chloroform to knock somebody out; that action would be direct and personal. None of the cited case law came anywhere close to what my suspect was doing: selling a legal substance knowing it was going to be abused and then taking advantage of the people who were abusing it.

I went to all the corrupting-children sections of the city and the problem was that the suspect did not have the duty to care for these kids. He was not a guardian, parent, or a person in authority. I began to feel maybe the detectives and administration were right. There was no readily apparent accessible provision in the *Criminal Code* to apply in this situation; at least not in the first and second read-throughs.

It was then I came across section 180. I think I may have skipped over it during my previous reading because I had never heard of anyone being charged with 'creating a common nuisance' before. Even now, thirty-two years later, I can remember how I felt. This obscure section of the *Criminal Code* was — I hoped — a potential solution to a problem that, until then, only a few recognized or were willing to accept to be a problem. Section 180 of the *Criminal Code* reads:

> Common nuisance
> - 180 (1) Every person is guilty of an indictable offence and liable to imprisonment for a term of not more than two years or is guilty of an offence punishable on summary conviction who commits a common nuisance and by doing so, (a) endangers the lives, safety or

health of the public, or (b) causes physical injury to any person.

Using my tried and true two-finger method, I typed an 'Information to Obtain' and a search warrant, using all the information I had collected to this point. 'Search warrant vetting' by supervisors — a policy within most police services where a supervisor approves a search warrant before it can be presented to a judge — may have been policy in 1989. If it was, I was not aware of it. I had done several search warrants and no one had ever called me to task over the content or quality of them. As it was with this particular warrant, I think if it had been reviewed, I believe I would have been shut down.

I nervously attended the Provincial Court and, search warrant in hand, proceeded directly toward the judge's chambers. As the clerk took the warrant to the judge, I sat and wondered if the judge would even entertain my assertion, that my suspect was breaking the law by providing a legal substance to people who were willingly using it and therefore responsible for causing them harm. Most people have no idea of the process of obtaining a search warrant. You can't explain it to the judge; you are presenting the information in written form and then asking the court to grant it — you hand over the 'Information to Obtain' and the Search Warrant to the judge and he reads it. It was a one-shot affair and everything has to be there on the document. Warrant-writing has become a specialized skill since 1989 and good warrant writers are an essential part of all investigative teams.

After a few tense minutes, the clerk led me into the judge's chambers and without comment, the judge asked me to swear to the information and then signed the warrant. His only words to me were, "Good luck, Constable." It was a very good start, but I wasn't there yet.

The next trick was getting enough help to execute the warrant. I had just been warned about tying up patrol resources for search warrants the week earlier after conducting a stolen property warrant. It was actually a double warning because the detectives said I had pre-empted their authority as they were working on the same case. I was supposed to check with them before doing warrants.

Most of the experienced patrol constables liked doing search warrants, and they also had a sense of what I was trying to do because they too were dealing with the sniffers. Search warrants beat out having to take 'theft from vehicles' and 'break-and-enter' reports during the day shift. And besides, if anyone got into trouble over this, it would be me; I was the one who got the warrant. So, after a quick meeting in the parking lot to come up with a plan, we went to the suspect's address. The suspect and five other people, three of them youths, were there. Everyone was high on lacquer thinner and the suspect mumbled there was no law against what they were doing. He probably genuinely believed this because he had been doing the same thing for years before I came along.

Everything the kids said would be there, was. Cans of lacquer thinner, small glass juice containers, all sorts of medications made out to people who were not present, were readily visible. Everyone was sorted out and I arrested my suspect. He started struggling when we were at the top of a long set of stairs. Knowing how many lives he had ruined and would continue to if left to his own devices, he picked a bad place to pick a fight. I could feel his hate. He was devoid of conscience and evil to me. He made it to the Saskatoon Police detention centre in good order. Then, in keeping with how things were going within my service for me at the time, the detention Corporal refused to book the suspect, saying he had never heard of the charge. There was a heated exchange between us which ended when I trumped his argument with the judge's signed warrant. The Corporal told me I would not last long with my attitude.

Suspect Lodged, Court Pending
After my suspect was lodged in a jail cell, I began the long process of exhibiting the material I had seized before completing my report. I had no idea what would happen in court the next day. How would the Crown prosecutor deal with this — or would he even proceed? How would the defence lawyer react? What would the judge in the courtroom, where first appearances are made, say? I was switching over to nights, so I would not know until I got back.

I don't know the exact sequence of events that took place or the details of how it unfolded, but God bless everyone involved. When faced with a period in remand after the initial arrest, the suspect pleaded guilty to creating a common nuisance and was sentenced to a year in jail. The local paper wrote a short story, and the arrest came to the attention of the Police Service Administration. The Police Service was portrayed in a positive light so I did not face any trouble for stirring the pot again.

With this win under my belt, now the real work started. I began re-interviewing some of the kids I suspected were abused by my suspect. It was difficult because of the misplaced loyalty they had to him, their addictions and, in some cases, the lasting effects of solvent abuse which had impaired their cognitive abilities. Within a couple of weeks, I had laid charges of sexual assault and sexual interference on this man. He had no preference for gender and abused both. I did this entirely on my own and was never offered any assistance or advice from anyone except encouragement from my fellow patrol members.

The local paper in Saskatoon, *The Star Phoenix*, printed more stories when the charges were laid. I did not realize it at the time but the paper was my best ally back then, bringing this otherwise largely ignored problem out into the public eye. I was at the station leaving a report on a day shift when one of the Sergeants came to me. He said the head of the Morality Unit was at the daily briefing with the Chief of Police and other senior administrators; he was taking credit in the paper for his detectives making the arrests. The Sergeant asked if this pissed me off. I told him I didn't care as long as my 'Pied Piper' was off the streets and in jail. I was not there for the glory. I was there to make a difference.

During my testimony, the suspect kept staring at me and pointing to his head then at mine. I knew he had shot himself in the head years before and I knew he was indicating that was what he was going to do to me.

Laying charges and successfully prosecuting offenders is sometimes very difficult when your witnesses are reluctant to come to court for a hundred different reasons. In the end, I secured only one conviction against my suspect which netted him a two-and-a-half-year sentence for sexually assaulting a boy from the same Reserve he was from.

During my testimony at one of the preliminary hearings, the suspect kept staring at me and pointing to his head then at mine. I knew he had shot himself in the head years before and I knew he was indicating that was what he was going to do to me. The presiding judge asked me what I thought, because he had witnessed the gestures too. I told him what I knew: Threats in court are very subjective, and in spite of this, I believe everyone knew what was going on but there was nothing anyone could really do about it.

There were a crazy number of things going on out on the streets throughout this period of time, but this case was especially important to me. I had many more difficult and controversial cases as my career went on, but this sniffing story is the one that immediately came to mind when I undertook to write a story for this book because of the lasting impact it had.

Other officers used my template for the common nuisance charges to take out other adult males who were providing lacquer thinner to youths. It took about two years of hits and misses before solvent abuse ceased to be a problem in Saskatoon. Between 1987 and 1991, a lot of people, including youths, died by misadventure, substance abuse, suicide, or murder. Many more are still dealing with the long-term neurological effects of solvent abuse to this day, but by 1991, except for the occasional diehard adult addicts, the issue of solvent abuse in Saskatoon was done. I take great pride in my contributions to bringing this to a satisfactory end.

Mission Driven
In the military, especially the combat arms, one tends to get very mission-driven; I certainly was. I saw a problem and worked on it until it was done. This case cemented the way I policed; though, I believe it was already in the mold just waiting to solidify. The indifference to this form of abuse was certainly a motivator; challenging indifference became a central theme through much of my career. Challenging leaders to lead. I avoid the term 'racism' because once you say that word, it causes people to turtle; they get defensive and dig in deeper. No change occurs this way. Indifference and racist attitudes are close cousins and leaders need to be on guard, always, and recognize neither is acceptable.

With the exception of a fifteen-month stint in the Street Crimes Unit, I ended up spending my entire career in patrol.

I worked in the central and west part of Saskatoon and was, as much as a cop could be, part of the community. I was a consistent presence, which — depending on what side of the law you were on — was either a good or a bad thing. Towards the end of my career, I often would tell stories that were based on my experiences. I used this as a leadership technique to individual constables and would wind up with an audience of several people. On more than a few occasions, they ended with one of the constables saying, "Sarge, you should write a book." So, write a book I did!

I avoid the term 'racism' because once you say that word, it causes people to turtle; they get defensive and dig in deeper. No change occurs this way.

As it was, I knew I had reached capacity for my ability to deal with trauma and its cumulative effects. I always believed when you say the words, I am going to retire, you are 'done'. I started writing my first book on my back deck. Handwritten in Hilroy old-school exercise books, the stories started to come together until eventually I had the workings of my first book. My general-purpose form went in after I found a publisher, and I retired from policework in 2013.

Since then, I have written three books and spoken to thousands of people from all walks of life about leadership and my experiences. It helped me to deal with the effects of the job and, in retrospect, I now see clearly what a violent world I had lived in. I found myself more relaxed and contemplative now. Almost every ex-police officer can tell you after leaving whatever force they were on, we never really see the world exactly the same way again. There is a depth of knowledge about people in all sorts of circumstances which remains imprinted. Sometimes cynical, but more often than not, accepting and just a little bit wiser, acknowledging no one is perfect and there are more good people than bad. The job carries on without you.

In 2019, retired for six years, I was in a Sobeys store in Saskatoon with my wife when a woman started walking toward us very purposefully. This situation can be unsettling; as all ex-police officers can tell you, it is hard to keep track of all of the people you have dealt with over your career. Angry people can just appear seemingly out of nowhere to give you the gears over something you had been involved in years before. This lady stopped short and asked, "Are you the guy who wrote the book, Indian Ernie?" I said I was. She explained she was a public health nurse in the centre of the area with the highest number of solvent abusers in the late 1980s and early 1990s. She said staff was overwhelmed with cases and then it seemed, all of a sudden, it was done. She never knew what happened until she read my first book. She thanked me and left. We drove home, smiling.

Lead whenever you can.

Debbie McGreal-Dinning is a former police officer with Hamilton Police Service. Following her time as a frontline patrol officer, she was seconded to Crime Stoppers, the Media Relations Office and the Domestic Bail Safety Unit where she was promoted to Sergeant. She also worked as a detective in the Criminal Investigations Division before leaving in 2016. Her journey has taken her out of law enforcement and into a healing space where she now supports women working in emergency services, providing backup in a different way. Deb continues to reside in her hometown of Hamilton with her husband and two children.

10

THE HOUSE WITH
THE LITTLE GREEN DOOR

■ ■ ■

Debbie McGreal-Dinning

Looking back over my career in law enforcement, it's the innocent, everyday calls that have sunk their teeth into me, rather than the complex and traumatic ones. Memories of these everyday calls pop up when I least expect it, slither their way into dreams and lie in wait in the recesses of my mind. A smell, an image, a word, a sound — like a wave they wash over me, and then just as quickly as they appear, they quietly recede, only to return another time, typically unannounced. Sadly, these so called 'everyday' calls are ones that take up the police board on any given shift day or night, sometimes based on misinformation, sometimes legitimate where in addition to police services being needed, so are the services of Child Protection.

Unified in Blue
Becoming a police officer and putting on a uniform unifies us in blue but does not erase who we are behind the badge. We all still carry our own stories and experiences that inevitably shape us into the beautiful, imperfect people we are, each person with a story equally unique to the next. The humanness that we carry behind the uniform is not frozen in time once we pull on our duty belts. It is what

we bring to the job as individuals that walks with us as we navigate our way through difficult, heartbreaking and dark experiences, given to us as both a gift and a burden. If we are to believe there can be no light without the dark, then we also know that in our careers in law enforcement, alongside the dark there are moments of light. This light refuels our strength and resilience, enabling us to show up when those in need call.

I answered countless calls that play out in my mind to this day. They all stayed with me in one way or another, some light and some darker than the midnight sky.

Being hired with the Hamilton Police in September of 2001 was one of the greatest accomplishments and proudest times in my life. Over the next sixteen years, I answered countless calls that play out in my mind to this day. They all stayed with me in one way or another, some light and some darker than the midnight sky, all adding a piece to the mind map of memories built over a career in law enforcement.

Heading into any shift, one grapples with the unknown, a shift wide open, no way of knowing what one will be faced with, waiting for the stories of the night to make themselves known. Over the air, your unit, your beat is called, and this starts the next twelve hours of your life. Coffee in hand, you are dispatched to a Child in Need call, one of the perhaps many on the board and most definitely not the only one for the night. My backup on this night is my squad mate and friend Jeff, already parked beside me. We are taking a breather, catching up on notes for the first ten-plus calls of the night, and it is not even midnight. Before hitting enroute (a button on our MDT's to advise our Dispatcher that we are on the way to the call), we take one last sip of our already 'iced' coffee, once hot at the start of the shift, but no longer. Information received while on the way to the call is minimal but just that someone wishing to remain anonymous had called concerned for the well-being of three little girls believed to be left alone at home.

Jeff and I pull up in front of the brown brick home on the corner of Cannon and Sanford Ave. almost simultaneously, go 10-17 (on scene) before exiting our cruisers. Our dispatcher advises that the apartment door, #3, is at the side of the house. Stepping away from the cruiser, I hear the brittle iced-over snow cracking under my boots and see my breath in the air as we both do a scan of the house before walking single file down the narrow, makeshift sidewalk leading to the crooked green door on the west side of the address. Tonight, Jeff is walking in front of me towards the door, making our bodies smaller as we move in the darkness between the brick exterior of the two old Hamilton homes. We both look down intermittently at our feet making sure not to lose our footing while navigating around ripped, open garbage bags and old soggy diaper boxes that did not make it to the curb for pick up. As we reach the door, instinctively we both lean in, listening for anything inside. These small movements and moments of rapport come instinctively to most officers — a look, a head nod, a breath — moving moment to moment like mirror images of each other. We hear nothing except for the humming sound of the Cannon bus, on the last run of the night. As we stand inches away from the faded green door, the streetlights no longer illuminate our cold breath. Our breathing is calm and controlled. After all, this is not a gun call, a robbery, or a homicide. It is a 'routine' call, or so we think, about three little girls, possibly in need of our assistance.

We move into position to knock on the little green door. I feel the frigid winter air seeping through my boots as I wiggle my toes around to ward off the cold. Standing on either side of the door frame, making sure not to stand directly in front of the door itself, I reach out and knock three times. Again, our bodies like mirror images of each other lean in to take another listen. Without having to say anything, I know Jeff too has heard what I have heard. We hold our breath for a moment and take a closer listen to what appears to be the soft, sweet and scared voices of little girls. I can hear one of them shush the others, instructing them to go watch TV.

The door slowly opens, and I can make out the slim silhouette of a little girl with golden blonde hair....
I can make out the pale, coloured flowers on her pajamas and also see the look of concern on her face.

She is direct with her words but I can hear the quivering of her voice and feel the fear of an eleven-year-old behind the sound of her voice. We can no longer hear voices behind the door so I reach over and knock once more softly, knowing that the little girl we are about to meet is standing directly on the other side. The door slowly opens, and I can make out the slim silhouette of a little girl with golden blonde hair. The little landing where she stands is in darkness but the light from the kitchen, three steps below, shines from behind. I can make out the pale, coloured flowers on her pajamas and also see the look of concern on her face. Through her eyes, before any words are spoken, I can see her mind racing for the story, for the lie she has been made to rehearse. They come more easily to her now as this is not the first time she has heard the knock on the door to find two uniform officers waiting.

As I begin to tell the little girl why we are there and ask if we can come inside, I can feel Jeff's slight body movements to my left, movements that may go undetected by someone not wearing a blue uniform. I know that he is looking beyond the landing and into the apartment. His safety scan of the apartment we are about to walk into goes unnoticed by the little girl, as she keeps her eyes on mine and reluctantly invites us into her home. As we walk beyond the green door, creating distance from the now not-so-faint smell of rot coming from the garbage bags, we are immediately met with the unmistakable odour of pet feces. The thick stink, attaching itself to our uniforms with each additional step into the basement apartment, becomes a backdrop to the call after only a few minutes.

I am grateful to be at this call with Jeff, he is kind, methodical and experienced. I also know he has a little girl at home waiting for him — he is both a cop and a daddy. A few years from this night, I will also have little ones of my own, a boy and a girl…

I look over at my partner as we now stand in the dimly lit kitchen with the golden-haired little girl standing in front of us, whom I will call Katy. Katy is trying to appear 'okay' while nervously wringing her hands, tugging on her flowered nightgown, and petting the head of their newest family member, a gentle brown lab, who loyally stands at her side. This has been his home from the streets for only a week or so but as he looks up at me with his light brown eyes, there is no mistaking that these three little girls are now his people. Jeff, with a kind smile and soothing voice, introduces himself. I can see the concern on his brow, with no words spoken, we both know how this little girl's night is going to go. As I take Katy into the living room to see her two sisters, I leave Jeff to check on the food situation and other necessities. I look back from the living room as he holds the fridge open for me to see. It is empty except for a large container of Kraft smooth peanut butter, and what looks like a pot. A peek inside later reveals day-old Kraft dinner, the little orange noodles sticking to the side, barely enough for one bowl. I stay with the girls as he continues into the bathroom. Later in the night, I hear him describing the tiny five-by-six-foot room to the Child Services worker over the phone, providing our assessment so they can then determine whether their attendance is required. No running water and a bathtub full of dog poop — no place for the girls to bathe is how it is about summed up.

I do not have to tell the little girl my story or that my heart oozes with understanding and empathy because of it. There is an unspoken knowing that transpires between the two of us.

My attention now back with little golden-haired Katy, she starts to tell me that her mom only went out for a minute to get groceries and that she would be home soon. Her eyes dart from left to right, up and down, searching for the lie, the lie she has had to tell many times before. Watching her tell such a complete and almost-believable lie, I see my own life reflected. So many lies, I get it. I was that little girl once upon a time, protecting my mother regardless of how sick she was, how neglectful, how high, how drunk, how gone. I often lied to my police officer father to protect my mother and our little broken world. She was my mother and the cover up and loyalty in my young mind was a matter of life and death.

I do not have to tell the little girl my story or that my heart oozes with understanding and empathy because of it. There is an unspoken knowing that transpires between the two of us. I am no longer a stranger, uninvited into her one-room basement apartment. As the night unfolds, she somehow finds the courage to trust and to slowly start telling the truth. As she and I sit on the edge of the one piece of furniture in the room, a double mattress, loosely covered with a Dora the Explorer blanket, she begins to talk. Her two little sisters seemingly forget about the two uniform officers in their home. They sit atop a large, lopsided cardboard box placed directly in front of a small flatscreen television and continue watching *The Wiggles*.

Katy starts to tear up as her tiny little voice confesses to not really knowing where her mommy is, but that she has not been home since the night prior. With every little piece of truth, she follows it up with a defence of her mommy's love for her. This back and forth reveals her sheer fear of telling the truth as it equals a betrayal of her mother and a terrifying disruption into their little world.

Witnessing her courage with every little word takes me back to an early winter morning in my own parents' west mountain townhouse, sitting at that kitchen table in the dark with Echo Beach by Martha and the Muffins playing in the background — a distant but crystal-clear memory of me rocking my little sister on my lap in the dark, lying to her as I told her mommy would be back soon, that she was just at work. I continued to lie, the truth was I had no idea where my mother had gone or why the front door was left wide open at four a.m. I was scared but the lie made me feel better. I would have been a few years younger than the little girl sitting beside me now, consoling my little sister during one of my mom's episodes where she had simply disappeared in the night. If police or even my father had shown up at the townhouse on that day and the others to follow throughout the years, I too would have lied. I am not sure I would have found the courage to follow up with the truth like the little one sitting beside me. The inner conflict of children in these situations is the belief that the telling of a lie will keep them safe, protect mom, keep them in their homes, bathtub full of dog poop or not. The only home they know.

She tells me that the last time this happened, they went to live with grandma in the country for a while. Exhausted, she looks up at me and asks me, "Is grandma coming to get us tonight?" I am unable to give her an answer at this point. I look over at Jeff who is now sitting at the kitchen

---

The truth is that I do not know how the night is going to play out but having been at so many calls like this, I had some inclination, and it makes my heart hurt.

---

table where he has carved out a small space amongst the plates crusted over with day-old ketchup and an ashtray running over with stale cigarette butts. Seemingly unaffected, he writes in his notebook while coordinating with Children's Aid.

With mom still not home and no one knowing her whereabouts, I continue to get to know this little soul a bit more. Looking weary, Katy continues to humour me, answering random questions about school, and the puppy they just took off the streets. She is concerned about her pup and expresses that she does not know if grandma will want to take him in on this night, if they end up with her. I try to assure her that everything will be okay and that we won't forget about her fur baby. The truth is that I do not know how the night is going to play out but having been at so many calls like this, I had some inclination, and it makes my heart hurt. Looking to change the subject, I look at the dirt-stained wall in front of us and see a lone dress loosely draped over a hanger. Like a piece of wall art, the pink plastic hanger balances on a single silver nail, displaying the once pure white dress. The light lacy material, now an off white, having been washed one too many times with random dark socks, has not yet been worn by the little girl. She explains that her mommy bought it for her recently, to be worn for her grade 6 graduation in the distant future. I hear gratitude and pride in her voice. Watching her face light up as she looks up at the dress, I tell her I love it and that she is surely going to look so very beautiful in it one day soon.

The quiet apartment soon begins to fill up as a Children's Aid worker joins us and grandma arrives not too far behind. The two youngest girls leave their cartoon for a moment, run over to the dimly lit kitchen and throw themselves into the arms of their mommy's mother. She is relieved to be there; she looks up from hugging the girls and takes inventory of the one-room apartment. Her gaze is brought back to the little girls as one of them jumps up and down begging her to take them to McDonald's … this scene has been played out before. Out of earshot of the girls, grandma tells us about her daughter's battle with drugs and alcohol, her history of disappearing for days on binges. She takes a deep breath in and with a sorrowful sigh, admits that she thought her daughter had really kicked it this time and that she was going to be okay, that this time it was going to be different.

I leave grandma for a moment and turn to Katy. When I look back at her, barely able to stay awake, I can tell she has heard it all — that she has known for weeks mom was not okay, but had also hoped this time would be different. It is now closing in on 2 a.m. She slowly gets up and starts to pack a little backpack for herself and her sisters.

With the little ones still wrapped around grandma's legs, I ask her if there is any way that the puppy they just rescued, or more fittingly the puppy that just rescued them, is able to come and stay. She does not look pleased at the thought, but her grand babies are everything to her and putting them through any more loss would kill her.

As Jeff and I continue to exchange information with grandma and the case worker, I feel a little tug at the back of my vest. Before I could turn around fully, I feel Katy's tiny arms hugging me around my waist. I hold her, thank her for being so brave, assure her that everything will be okay before watching her walk out the little green door and into the night with her sisters and her puppy by her side.

Jeff and I return to our cruisers, drive away from the Cannon Street address and find a quiet place to park to do our report, sipping on our now freezing cold coffees. The smell of dog poop and old cigarettes float up from our uniforms. Thinking back now, we probably went on to attend several more calls that night and ones that may have been even more serious or involved. But the call I remember on that night is the one with the little dress hanging lifeless on that smoke-stained wall and a brave little girl who loved her mommy regardless of her brokenness. I never saw that little girl again but close to twenty years later, I can still hear Katy's little voice, see her defiant sad eyes, wonder if she got a chance to wear her pretty white dress and pray that she rose out of the brokenness to write her own story of resilience.

My Own Story of Resilience
Part of my map, my journey to choosing Law Enforcement, I believe, was through osmosis, growing up with my father as a police officer. One of my earliest memories was of a staunch blue uniform, seeing the intricate design of the Hamilton flash, all blue, white and red on the shoulder of my dad's long police issued winter coat. I can still feel the

cold, crispness of the blue material against my cheek, the mysterious and sometimes haunting smell of the streets coming to life from the coat to my nose. I think at this time my parents were still together, so at three years old, seeing the duty belt slung over the headboard of the bed, the worn in and cracked black leather of the holster, will forever be images that come easily to me. Thinking back now, there were so many moments which greatly impacted me, guided me, and tattooed on me, my path and eventual decision to become a police officer.

This path, however, almost did not happen for me. It is twenty years since I sat in the lobby of the police service-appointed psychiatrist in Toronto. This stage of the hiring process was a two-hour-long question period with someone who had been chosen to assess our mental readiness. Looking up from my *Cottage Life* magazine, I saw the psychiatrist look up from her notepad and motion that I was next. Walking into her office at 29 years old, I felt uneasy, with the beads of sweat rolling down the back of my neatly pressed button-down shirt. Her office was small with a leather couch and chair and a window letting just enough light in to remind me of the scorching sun outside.

She asked many questions over that two-hour period coupled with even more silent pauses as she diligently scribbled down what I can only assume were my responses. To this day I can only recall one question from my time with her and that is only because my response was a transparent "Yes." it was also the only time I remember her looking up from her notebook, eyeglasses pulled down over nose, the only time I felt her really look at me.

The question was, "Has anyone in your family struggled with alcohol or substance abuse?" Assuming all potential hires were asked the same, I answered openly and honestly. Looking back down at her notes, she carried on writing as I detailed my mother's struggle with both alcohol and prescribed drugs for most of my life — it only really coming to an end for when I left for university in Ottawa at nineteen. Truth be told, the dependencies have never really ended for her.

The psychiatrist then went on to ask if I had sought any counseling and the like over the years, which without putting much thought towards the response, I answered truthfully, "No, I have not." I explained that my version of counseling was moving away from home for school, living across Canada in British Columbia and later in my twenties living and teaching English in South America, which for me was healing of a different kind. I was confident and sincere in 'explaining' my journey with wellness but also felt that my single mother's struggle with substance abuse over the years, and me stationed early in life as her caregiver, had only made me stronger, more resilient, more compassionate, and fit to serve. I earnestly communicated to her that my lived experience was not something I ever considered a detriment to wearing the uniform. I believed it to be a benefit, and that such a life would only, in my opinion, make me a better cop. She listened, jotted down some more notes, reluctantly agreed with me but not before once again pulling her glasses down across the middle of her nose. She warned that this lived experience, or maybe the not-seeking-counseling piece, I am not sure which, would one day, as she put it, "Bite me in the ass."

Creating a Healing Space
Throughout my career, I would hear the warning of that psychiatrist come up several times, her thoughts about my not getting her version of counseling because of my mother's drug and alcohol struggles and proclaiming that it would bite me in the ass one day. Looking back over twenty years, I have come to agree with her, but not in the way I think she intended. From the time I left home at 19 for university,

to the time I returned at 28 years old, I made myself go to places that allowed me to become intimate with the dualities of this life — shame and worthiness, love and loathing, confusion and clarity, fear and courage. This was very messy at times, but I moved through those valleys, a student of life, the human way, the way most of us must go to figure out who we are and what we are made of, both the light and the dark, a journey not a destination. For so many, we are not running or attempting to bypass the painful parts, we are simply breathing, moving, embracing the brokenness, and seeing ourselves in a new way out of the shards. Sometimes it is not necessary to get fixed, it is not necessary to be all put back together, glued together — sometimes a piece is good enough. Now more than ever with social media showcasing carefully constructed snippets of others' lives, we are made to focus on perfection and whole things, when nothing can truly be whole. I believe we can still be beautiful in our brokenness.

How I showed up that night for Katy and her sisters was largely a result of my own lived experience, my own resiliency out of brokenness. If feeling, reflecting, connecting, empathizing, hurting, showing up vulnerable, courageous and imperfect as a police officer means that you have fallen short or allowed some part of who you are and where you have come from to bite you in the ass, then yes, she was right, that happened. Responding to the countless calls over the years, I would not have wanted it any other way. I do not think the people I have had the honour of serving with in Hamilton over the years, many times in their darkest moments, would have either.

A few years ago, I made one of the most difficult decisions in my life. I chose to leave my policing career. Since this time, I have come to embrace the notion that to heal, we need to look everywhere, both traditional and alternative. Every form of support and help is vital on its own and yet so incomplete. A police officer's job is complex, your backup needs to reflect this, and support systems need to be available from multiple areas and traditions. It takes a village. Being on the outside over these almost-five years and having the opportunity of looking back in, I began to investigate this intricate mind map of ours and how we store memories and trauma. My journey has taken me out of law enforcement and into a healing space where I now provide back-up in a different way. Many in law enforcement continue to struggle in silence — the stress and trauma residing in our hearts, minds and bodies, along with a belief that somehow acknowledging this part of us makes us failures. Struggling mentally and emotionally because of the work we do and the things we have seen does not make us weak, it makes us human.

It is my great honour and focus to now hold a lantern, to create a space to help police officers see through the fog and shine a light on a way forward. It is my hope to contribute to a healing space with my writing and with Blue Heart Healing (bluehearthealing.com). My mission with this work is to combine all areas of my certification including trauma-focused Neuro-linguistic programming, Time Line Therapy, Core Transformation, and Eco-Therapy, and to create a connectedness, providing a space for those in law enforcement to feel seen, valued, and validated. This focus has also led to me create a self-guided journal dedicated to police officers, a journal that is full of thoughtful prompts to identify triggers which cause stress and discomfort. My intention is to gently guide officers towards a myriad of anxiety reduction strategies, learn effective self-soothing, and mindful connection to healing.

My continued life's work is to support those in law enforcement by being a connector, to provide a space of stillness and calm, to help officers look everywhere for light, both outward and inward, to help them find a way that builds inner strength instead of outer dependencies, to find deep love for the person behind the uniform. This is an unending process, not a destination. By shining a light on our imperfections and our humanness, it is my hope that others will feel safe and supported to do the same. Silence and complacency will only continue to deepen the feelings of shame and the fear that so many carry with them as being weak. This narrative is killing our officers and holding them back from connecting their truest self, to who they are at the core — the person behind the badge.

David Wilton proudly served with the Saskatoon Police Service for almost 33 years. His duties included time in patrol, traffic, drugs, and youth. David had quite a variety of very interesting cases — some shocking. The death of a friend and fellow officer, killed in the line of duty, reminded him of just how dangerous police work can be. There were many highlights in his career, but one stands out above the rest — and that was the apprehension of child killer David Threinen.

11

MISSING AND MURDERED CHILDREN

■ ■ ■

David Wilton

POLICEWORK is not for everyone. But it was for me. I was born in London, England during World War II to an English war bride and a Canadian anti-tank soldier. We came to Canada and settled in Regina, Saskatchewan in 1946 and I had my schooling there. While in high school, I decided I wanted to be a policeman and signed up as soon as I was old enough. Saskatoon and its police service attracted me, so that is where I went.

I started with the Saskatoon Police Service in January of 1965. After training classes, I was assigned to patrol and traffic, in uniform. In those early years, I walked the beat and dealt with traffic and accidents. In 1970, I was assigned to work with the RCMP Drug Unit. While so assigned, I had many occasions to team up with their Major Crime Unit, General Investigation Section. They were a great bunch to work with; smart and dedicated to law enforcement.

Missing Children
The summer of 1975 in Saskatoon was typical, with many warm days and plenty of rain. So much rain, in fact, the South Saskatchewan River running through Saskatoon was high and flowing very fast. Citizens were cautioned to stay away from the river as it was dangerous the way it was.

In mid-June of that summer, two children went missing. Twelve-year-old Dahrlyne Cranfield and nine-year-old Robert Grubesic had gone bike riding and their bikes were found abandoned on the banks of the South Saskatchewan River. There was no sign of the children, and at first, there was speculation perhaps they had fallen into the river and were swept away. That possibility was very real, with their bikes found so close to the raging river.

We went through literally thousands of reports, looking for any files involving children or attempts to abduct children. That work, though exhausting, paid off.

Days went by with no sign of the missing children. A team of police officers had been assembled and assigned to the case, and I was on that team. As Saskatoon was not a huge city population-wise, it was not surprising I knew the father of the missing girl, Daye Cranfield. He was a local businessman and a real gentleman. I felt his pain and worry, especially whenever I met or spoke with him. We could not offer many words of encouragement because we had so little to go on.

In short order, we realized we had a serious problem on our hands. No time was wasted as the Saskatoon Police Chief arranged for our team to work together with the Saskatoon RCMP Major Crimes Unit, General Investigation Section. All local-known sex offenders and child molesters were identified and located. Each was questioned thoroughly and all alibis were checked out and investigated.

Two More Missing Children

The local media were very cooperative and, naturally, very interested. The media were asked to help, and help they did. They put out a plea for the public's assistance and encouraged them to call the police with any information or tips. And Saskatoon's public did just that—many tips were called in and checked out. Nevertheless, Saskatoon had never experienced a serial child killer before and the citizens were not willing to seriously consider we had one now.

The police assigned to this case, as mentioned, were a combination of Saskatoon Police Service and RCMP investigators. We worked well together, as we had often put our heads together on different matters and crimes, and it was quite common to find an RCMP member teamed up with a Saskatoon Police Service officer. Occasionally, a lead would take them outside of Saskatoon and by working together, jurisdiction was not an issue; the RCMP had federal authority and Saskatoon Police had provincial authority.

As we entered the month of July, there was still no sign of the missing children. Suddenly, two more children were missing: Samantha Turner, age eight, and Cathy Scott, age seven. These girls had been playing in a playground on the east side of the city, an area that was quite different than the area where the first two children went missing. Saskatoon's east side was searched thoroughly, to no avail. The media pleaded with the public to call the police with any information they might have.

We went through literally thousands of previous reports, looking for any files involving children or attempts to abduct children. That work, though exhausting, paid off— we were able to find other instances where someone had tried to pick up children. Thankfully, those attempts had been unsuccessful and those children lived to tell the details, and because of this we were able to compose a drawing of the suspect in addition to unearthing details of his clothing and car. This provided us with a good idea of what our suspect might have looked like.

By this time, the City of Saskatoon was on the verge of panic. I could feel it. There were four children missing, and we were now into August. I could only imagine the agony the parents were going through. Frustration reigned and people were reluctant to let their children out of sight. I was worried, too, as I was a relatively new father, having a four-year-old son and a six-year-old daughter at home. There were times I wished I were at home with them, rather than being out all hours looking for the four missing children, but I had a duty to fulfill and we wanted desperately to locate those children.

A Confession
Here we had four children missing, presumed to have been abducted and killed by an unknown person: Could we solve this mystery? Would we be removed and assigned to other cases? Is it possible we may never see a conclusion to this case, be it good or bad? Often, this was what happened. This uncertainty is a common thread among policework; we often just don't know.

Then, on a morning in August, we received a call that changed everything. The informant told us to check out David Threinen, who worked in a tire shop in downtown Saskatoon. We wasted no time locating Threinen. Even before questioning him, we felt we had our man! He closely resembled our composite drawing, and his car and clothing matched what we were looking for. Threinen even had a fringed leather jacket, which was specific clothing mentioned in several attempted abduction files.

We soon learned Threinen had been charged with the murder of a young girl in Lethbridge, Alberta a year or two earlier, but the charge had been dropped due to a legal technicality. Why didn't we know about that? I don't have an answer.

After being warned and having his rights explained to him, Threinen was taken to the Saskatoon Police Station and questioned. The investigators were top notch and knew what had to be done. Within a relatively short time, Threinen confessed to the crimes. He confessed to strangling each child and said a voice in his head told him to do it. He then agreed to take us to where the bodies had been left.

Obviously, Threinen had committed one of the worst crimes imaginable. The murder of four young children chills a person to the bone. We did not know, at that time, what he had done to these innocent children. It is hard to comprehend, but after having committed these horrendous crimes, Threinen went back to work and carried on as usual at the downtown tire shop.

David William Threinen, then age 27, directed our team to an area south of Saskatoon, just east of the South Saskatchewan River. The area was flat land with open fields, with the occasional clump of bushes or trees. He led us to a small clump of bushes and showed us the remains of the first two children who went missing. The children had been missing for over a month and were badly decomposed, as expected. The bodies were well hidden in the bushes.

Threinen then led us to a second location, this time north of the city limits. Again we were directed to a clump of trees and there we found the remains of the second pair of children who were missing for about two weeks. Decomposition had already begun. Autopsies conducted later revealed evidence of sexual assault on one of the three female victims, a devastating confirmation of our worst fears.

It was at this point we found ourselves in one of the

most difficult moments of anyone's life: having to notify the parents of what we had found. We all felt indescribable pain and sympathy for them. Words cannot describe their reaction. How did the parents feel? We could only imagine. It goes without saying they would have been forever devastated and heartbroken. When the terrible news was made public, Saskatoon citizens were in shock. This type of crime was unheard of, except in books and in the movies.

We had two young children at home and I can only imagine the torment and agony we would have experienced had our children been such victims.

Laying charges
Threinen was charged with four counts of murder contrary to Section 218(2) of *The Criminal Code of Canada*, punishable by life imprisonment. He went to trial in February 1976, held in Her Majesty's Court of Queen's Bench in Saskatoon. I was assigned to be at Threinen's side at all times, for his protection and the public's. During the proceedings, his confession was read out to the court. Then court had a short break and I took Threinen to a back room. There, I asked him what he thought when his confession was read out. Threinen looked at me, shook his head and said, "I wasn't listening. I was thinking about fishing up North." At the conclusion of the trial, Threinen was found guilty and sentenced to life in prison with no chance of parole for 25 years.

After serving almost 25 years, Threinen was eligible

for parole and given a hearing. At the parole hearing, he said he did not want parole and he did not want to be released. His parole was denied.

I did wonder how the parents felt about the sentence handed down to Threinen. I don't know for sure, as I was never informed. I do wonder why the court did not hand down consecutive life sentences, meaning four life terms, each one being 25 years. I also believe there is a place for capital punishment in Canada. This case in particular would have been a perfect case for such a penalty. Capital punishment should only apply when an accused has given a statement confessing to the crime, or if there is a credible eye witness to the offence. We had two young children at home and I can only imagine the torment and agony we would have experienced had our children been such victims. I have no doubt Threinen would have killed again had he not been caught and convicted.

A Career in Painting
In 1997, I retired from the Saskatoon Police Service as a superintendent, having served almost 33 years. Being only 53 years old, I knew I was too young to just sit around and do nothing. It is funny, but on day two — yes, the second day of retirement — my wife said, "You are not going to sit around here and do nothing. Go do something. You like to paint, so go paint!"

Luckily, I had greatly enjoyed painting walls and homes and had dealt with a paint store close to home. I told my wife I would go right away and see what they'd have to say. The owner welcomed me with open arms and offered me a good discount on paint and supplies, plus free advice. Right then I formed a business, "DW Painting," named after my initials. Knowing a couple of good painters, I asked them to work for me. One of the workers was a mother and the other was a university student. They accepted and we were out looking for work!

My wife was pleased, as I would soon be out of her hair — she was used to having the house to herself most of the time. Baking and cooking were high on her to-do list, with housekeeping not far behind. I still kept doing the yard work and shoveling snow. I hired a few painters and the next twenty years saw DW Painting doing full-time work, painting houses inside and out. We did very good work and had no complaints. We loved the interaction with people and the painting itself was a pleasure, and at times even fun.

Any time something is painted, it appears new.
The smell of fresh paint conjures images of
spring and summer and new beginnings.
The old and tattered look is shaken off and
sad becomes happy again.

I find painting therapeutic. Any time something is painted, it appears new. The smell of fresh paint conjures images of spring and summer and new beginnings. The old and tattered look is shaken off and sad becomes happy again. When someone paints a house, furniture is often moved or replaced. When a room is painted, it might be a different colour and the furniture may change location. The room often takes on an entirely different look. A fresh start.

For the painter, there is a little more to it. He or she can look at the work, see the end result and be proud of a job well done, or lament over one done poorly. It is similar to policework in many ways, with one notable exception: in policework, most officers never get to see the end result of their efforts. With painting, this retired officer finally has the satisfaction of enjoying the end result of a job well done.

Trish L. Haley is a retired Ottawa Police Officer. She joined the OPS in 1991 after obtaining an Associate of Arts in Criminal Justice from Camosun College. While serving with the OPS, she completed a Baccalaureate of Social Sciences in Criminology from the University of Ottawa. She's also a recipient of a Commendation Award presented by the OPS in 1993. Trish has four children and six grandchildren. In retirement, her passion for policework has been replaced with a passion for painting.

12

ADVENTURES ON D PLATOON

■■■

Trish Haley

Dear Angela Keara, my great-great-granddaughter,

Your world is 2080 and mine 2021. You're just beginning life and mine is closer to conclusion. Your hair is red and face filled with freckles, an Irish trait. Along with a temper and stubbornness, you never give up. Your name is Angela after my daughter, your great grandmother. Your middle name is Keara after my granddaughter, your grandmother. My name is Trish and I wish it were possible to meet you to pass on my experiences and decisions. My story about my Adventures on D Platoon will have to do, and all I ask is that you write a letter back to me and give them both to your daughter or son to keep this story alive.

In August 1991 I was hired by the Ottawa Police. I had applied at the encouragement of our then-chief, Chief Flanagan, after thinking over a phone conversation we'd had a few years earlier. He was a great man, honoured by the Ottawa Police Service on March 3, 1993 when they renamed the police headquarters the Thomas G. Flanagan Building, located at 474 Elgin Street.

At the time of my hiring, I had earned my diploma in

criminal justice from Camosun College in Victoria, British Columbia and I was working toward a social sciences degree at the University of Ottawa, majoring in criminal justice. After five weeks of class training at the Ottawa headquarters, my fellows and I were bustled off to the Ontario Police College, located near St. Thomas, Ontario and by February 1992, we'd received our badges and signed the Oath of Office. Our police recruiting class was the first in Canadian history comprised of so many women. We all felt the pressure to succeed. I was assigned to D Platoon consisting of thirty-two men and three women. *Angela, now I will share a call with you that changed my life forever.*

Never. Give. Up.
I don't recall the exact date this horrible incident occurred — sometime in the 1990s — but I will never forget it, or the suspect. And I will never forget that Cst. Marc Denis (his postscript follows mine in this chapter) and Cst. Joe Ieradi saved my life. Hopefully, my story sends this message to you: Never. Give. Up.

On an isolated Ottawa street, I pulled over a truck for a broken taillight. I remained in my cruiser and began checking the plate and running the name of the registered owner. As soon as I saw the name 'Frederick Koepke' on my mobile data terminal (MDT), I shuddered with fear. This same man, Frederick Koepke, had murdered a young constable by the name of David Kirkwood in 1977 during an incident where seven other officers had also been injured. Koepke was later found not guilty by reason of insanity and sent to a psychiatric facility. Ten years later, he was released into the public by way of a lifted Lieutenant Governor Warrant, a warrant that had been employed when Koepke was deemed to have been insane when he committed the murder.

By the time I pulled Koepke over for his broken taillight, I had already been warned about him by other

D Platoon officers: He was a very dangerous man, often high on cocaine, and he hated women. Coincidentally, the quiet Ottawa street was just around the corner from where the young constable David Kirkwood had been shot and killed. That may have, in part, accounted for my unusual fear and panic.

Before I could collect myself, Koepke had already leapt from his truck. He charged toward my cruiser and violently pounded his fists on the hood in an unhinged rage. In the headlights, his face was distorted and his yelling was filled with anger. He screamed, "I'm sick of you guys stopping me! I've had it!" He began to wave his arms frantically and I could see his eyes were glazed over and wild.

Instinctively, I rolled down the window and reached to pull my gun from the holster. The release clip was stuck. I was still in the driver's seat. Over the MDT, Joanne, the District 1 dispatcher, asked if all was '10-4' (okay). I froze. I can't recall my reply or the message sent via my MDT, nor did I remember to press the red emergency button. I was unable to leave my cruiser because Koepke was blocking the driver's door now. I needed time to find a solution, to calm him down, to take control of the situation.

I couldn't think straight. All I could muster was "10-4" into the radio clipped to my uniform. I should have called a "10-78" (emergency, officer needs assistance), but I didn't.

I knew I was in trouble. I tried rolling up the window but Koepke beat me to it, holding the window down as he continued to scream, "I've had it! I've had enough this time!" His words were slurred and his face was contorted with anger. There was foam around his mouth and his heated breath was foul. I could feel him breathing and spitting on my face. Voices of dispatch and other officers over the radio. Sirens. Winding down like a battery failing. All in slow motion. Then … stop. It was in this moment another unit arrived. A reflection of coloured lights in my rear-view mirror; shadows bouncing toward the sky. A tear spilled from my eye over my cheek. My hand remained on my gun, as if it were glued in place. I couldn't release my grip. *Angela, I couldn't think straight.*

Emergency Response
Cst's. Marc Denis and Joe Ieradi had heard my voice over the radio and they knew I was in trouble. They were known as the Emergency Response Unit. When they ran my call and saw the name 'Koepke' they raced to the scene, a shotgun mounted between their seats. All I remember is the sound of a shotgun being racked and someone ordering Koepke to step away from my cruiser with his hands up. Still unable to move from the driver's seat or release the grip of my gun, more tears flowed. I wiped them away. I didn't want anyone to see.

Today I'm unable to recall how Koepke was dealt with. I don't remember if there was a court case; there must have been. All I do remember is being certain my life was over. That call, that shift… my last thought would be of my children, Danielle, Elliott, Andre and Angela, and my last words, "Tell my children I love them all." The road was dark, empty, and deathly quiet; just my cruiser and Koepke's truck. I sometimes wonder if he planned it that way, because it seemed to be too large of a coincidence for this to happen so closely to the house where Cst. Kirkwood was murdered.

I never told Cst. Marc Denis or Cst. Joe Ieradi how much I panicked. How I froze. I never told Marc or Joe I truly believed life was over. I've never told anyone I still have nightmares today. I never told Marc or Joe thank you for saving my life. I wish there were words to express my gratitude. In lieu of words, a painting for each of you will have to do. But Marc, remember, you still owe me $5,000! (You will need to read on to understand why).

Today I was thinking about Cst. David Kirkwood

and his pregnant wife, his murder, and their then-unborn daughter, who would've been about the same age as my son, Elliott, today. I don't know if she became a police officer, like her dad. They were all forefront in my mind when confronted by Koepke that night; how quickly one person changed three lives forever. If my recollection is accurate, Koepke had a list of officers' names found on him that were to become his targets. I don't want to think about how much worse that could've all ended, had Koepke not been apprehended. *Angela, I think Marc found a list of officers' names in Koepke's left-side shirt pocket. Koepke was wearing a stained white t-shirt and over it, an open shirt with a square pattern of yellow and black.*

"Don't Shoot Him!"
Later in my career I took a 911 complaint involving a gun in the same area, one street over from Bell Street. At that time, it was routine for the district to have frequent calls involving disputes, assaults and drugs. It reminded me of the Koepke call: tense, unpredictable, and challenging. Death, so close.

As I arrived on scene, I saw a young man in his late twenties matching the description of the suspect. The only information I had at this point was that he was on his way to get a gun from his parked car to shoot his neighbour. There was no time to park my cruiser; I left it in the street, motor running, and the driver's door remained open. I ran toward the suspect, pointing my .38 revolver and I ordered him to stop and to step away from his vehicle with his hands up — I needed to confirm he wasn't holding a gun. He wouldn't cooperate and continued toward his car.

Suddenly the suspect's mother ran out from a house, screaming, "Don't shoot my son! Please… don't shoot him!" Their dog began to bark. The suspect was startled by his mother's voice for a moment and he paused. The mother, now hysterical, continued to plead with me not to shoot her son. The scene was chaotic. I scanned the area quickly to ensure no one else was close to the activity, as the area is made up of houses and apartment blocks. The mother was still pleading and crying. In this moment my only focus was to make certain the suspect didn't open his car door, because if he retrieved that gun, there would be a standoff.

I put more pressure on the trigger.
I could feel the sting of sweat blurring my vision.
I had no cover and was under a streetlamp.
I was a target.

I put more pressure on the trigger. With the target in sight, I blocked the chaos; my mind sharpened with silent concentration. I could feel the sting of sweat blurring my vision. I had no cover and was under a streetlamp. I was a target. The radio was silent; someone must have called for a '10-3' (stop transmission). I repositioned myself on the street, moving closer to the car. I needed to be positive the suspect wouldn't open the car door. The young man's mother was crying out, again, "Please don't kill my son!" A dog was now at my heels, growling.

"Listen to your mother!" I yelled, hoping he would respond to something personal. I did not want to kill this young man, but he was adamant about retrieving his gun. He continued, his hand on the car door. Again, I ordered him to stop or I would shoot to kill — his choice.

The suspect placed his hand on the car door. He was preparing to open it. I positioned to shoot the target. A life. With the suspect's chest in my sights, I put more pressure on the trigger. I was just about to fire when suddenly, without warning, I heard an approaching car and saw flashing lights. I don't recall hearing sirens. Another unit had arrived on scene.

Using their cruiser doors for cover, they aimed their guns toward the suspect. "Stop! Get on the ground! Hands behind your head! Do it now!" Three guns were now positioned to shoot. We all ordered the suspect away from the car, one last chance: "Hands behind your head and to the ground!" The young man complied ... finally. I wiped the sweat from my forehead, relieved I didn't take his life.

The other unit, SWAT officers, later advised me there was a second guy residing in a house behind me who had my head in his sights, fixing to shoot me during the standoff. They inquired why I didn't wait for back up. My response? There was no time, no units free, and not enough patrol officers — a common problem in 1994, and a problem that still persists today. In that moment, however, I didn't care about the risk. *Angela, it was all part of the job.*

A Last Resort
A call like that is difficult and exhausting. As an officer you try to use your gun only as a last resort. It's not like target practice at the range in a controlled setting; you react, sometimes unpredictably. You hope to finish your shifts, return home to your family, and finally retire from a policing career without needing to take a life, or losing yours. My children's photos on my locker reminded me to have a safe shift; they were depending on my return home.

After that incident and the Koepke call, I was warned and tested constantly. I tended to take too many chances and a lot of simple calls became chaotic. The guys drilled it into my head a multitude of times. "Trish, your manner is dangerous." "Trish, you take too many chances." "Trish, you take too many risks." They tried to help by offering advice but I was stubborn — I had quite the attitude and that old

Irish temper. I was just trying to do a good job. I knew there was a lot to prove, particularly for a female officer. The Koepke case was a concern. So was the Bell Street gun call. *Angela, in situations like Koepke or the Bell Street call, life can end in a microsecond — the other officer's, the suspect's, or even mine.*

Not Enough Officers
Many calls and not enough officers was a normal state for District 1. After all, the location was downtown Ottawa and crime was growing. It was about this time when my son, Elliot, was hired for a job at Dunkin' Donuts in the area. I know. Troubling.

At the beginning of one of my shifts, a disturbance call came across the radio as I was leaving the garage. I hadn't even booked on yet. My greatest fears were realized when I heard the address of Dunkin' Donuts; I was concerned for Elliot's safety. I knew he was working because I had just dropped him off. My heart began to race as I sped to the shop. On scene, Elliot advised me of the problem: A patron refused to pay for his coffee and refused to leave. Elliot then pointed him out to me.

As I approached the suspect, I detected a familiar odour. He smelled of the street — body odour, stale liquor, and tobacco. When I inquired about what the problem was, he stood up sharply from his seat and attempted to hit me in the head with a cup. A fight ensued. A coffee cart smashed into a glass display. By that point, Elliot was already calling dispatch, telling them to hurry and send backup, "My mom's going to be killed!" Two more officers arrived, the suspect now in handcuffs, and Dunkin' Donuts…in complete shambles. Donuts and coffee… everywhere. *Angela, do you recall what I said? That in situations like Koepke, Bell Street, or even Dunkin' Donuts, life … can … end … in a microsecond?*

D Platoon

Angela, let me tell you about my good friends in D Platoon. I loved being part of D Platoon. When I was first assigned, I was one of only three female officers, and the guys taught me so much. Many became like brothers to me. They gave me good advice about surviving the streets, they taught me how to gather information on suspects, and they drilled home the importance of running licence plates during traffic stops (especially Cst. John Medeiros). They became my family.

Mike McGuire taught me to always trust my gut. He also did wicked John Wayne and Joe Pesci impressions. He even taught me how to barter at garage sales. On one occasion, I had purchased a huge round coffee table during my lunch break. I wedged it in the back of my cruiser, not able to fully close my trunk, and proudly drove back to the station. When two detectives observed my return to the garage, they turned to me and said, "You must work with McGuire." I motioned to the coffee table and responded, "Evidence." Mike taught me that, too.

Marc Denis, one of the two officers who came to my aid with the Koepke call, always made the job super fun. If you needed car repairs, just call and he'd be there in a flash. Come to think of it, I think he still owes me ten bucks; I have a photo to prove he was holding the ten bucks, but I never did receive it — so I figure, with compounded interest, that ten bucks should be about $5,000 today. Time to pay up, buttercup.

Joe Ieradi spent hours pumping iron at the gym. One look at his rippling muscles causes the bad guys to surrender. (I could really use a bodyguard right now, Joe, if you're in Kelowna and looking for a job.)

Timmy, well he was just hilarious. He was always digging through garage sale garbage after midnight, once even causing me to get a noise complaint to investigate. His intestinal gas was near lethal and could no doubt smoke out a bad guy to surrender, even when hidden under a mattress. It was so pungent it would cause K-9s to yelp and flee — even down a ladder during a commercial break-and-enter check. Yes, Tim, your gas is that potent. I have a great photo of Tim standing beside an Oscar Mayer van, the one parked in the Glebe with the giant wiener on top. In true form, he was holding his stomach. He was always eating, particularly between calls, and not just Dunkin' Donuts either — pizza, shawarma, Chinese food, hamburgers, 7-Eleven hot dogs that often looked expired, plus his game-meat sandwiches. It's really no wonder his gas smelled of death.

With Winston, my friend, we shared great Chinese food and sunrises over the Ottawa River trying to keep each other awake between calls. We bonded over stories of our grandfathers; how his grandfather, once a slave, escaped the United States to Canada on the underground railroad toward freedom, and how my grandfather travelled from Dublin to Canada, only to be greeted with angry mobs chanting "Irish Go Home!" (Ironically, many of those Irishmen became police officers.) Winston was Black and I, a white Irish woman. We both struggled for our positions and overcame a lot of adversity. Our talks helped more than I suspect he'll ever know. The unique sound of his laugh is a cherished memory. And good painting material...

Shawn we lost to suicide, an all-too-common outcome for officers who've been worn down by tragedy and left to navigate the landmines of PTSD, often without help. Oh I miss him dearly and wish I'd said more, tried a little harder. Our last conversation was in the garage; he was so desperately sad. It was a stupid call with a tragic end for both the suspect and Shawn and terribly unfair. He was criticized by many and tried to stay strong, but the darkness won and he could take no more. We lost Teddy, too. The pain in his eyes, the sadness of spirit. When we hugged goodbye, I had a bad feeling. Now both Shawn and Teddy are gone, forever.

Cst. Joe Droskie was an understanding, kind and compassionate man, and a good officer too. Joe worked hard and never complained about his leg. I don't know if he was shot, but he struggled to walk. He was an inspiration. He came to my rescue once, too, but not without first having a little fun. Now, before I continue, you have to understand Joe. He loved pranks. Especially Halloween pranks. Sometimes he had a morbid sense of humor; I believe it was his artistic escape, as painting is for me.

My first patrol of District 4 was on Halloween. I was guarding the Billings Estate Museum — a historical tourist attraction in the Village of Billings Bridge — which at the time sat empty and without power. Some time into my shift, I needed to use the washroom and the only one was inside the estate. I sent Joe a message on my MDT asking him to come to my location to accompany me inside. I was in a desperate situation — if you're a woman reading this, you know what I mean! Little did I realize, my request gave him the perfect opportunity to have a little 'fun'.

Joe arrived on scene just as the rain began — not softly, but a righteous downpour. We proceeded to the estate through mud, rain, and darkness. Using our flashlights, we fortunately found the kitchen and facilities quickly, but now I needed to deal with the 20 lbs of gear around my waist and a huge radio with its cord, in the dark, all the while trying to concentrate on the task at hand. That's when Joe began: He started with the ghosts calls, followed by stomping on stairs and floor. Then he yelled out, "Watch out for the spiders under the toilet seat! They bite!" Now, let me ask you: could you 'focus' under those conditions?

As I said, many of these guys were like brothers. They taught me so much and even though the job was challenging, they made me laugh. Eric was always telling me to relax and stop complaining, but with a smile. He never lost his cool — he didn't have to, because his size and quiet voice would cause even the biggest bad guys to surrender without hesitation. Then there was Guy, who always gave good old-fashioned advice (yes, Guy, I have finally cut my bangs and my hair isn't flat anymore).

Finally, there was Staff Sgt. Larry Hill. He understood I was having difficulty with my son and told me not to worry about booking off. He realized I was new to the platoon, but he made it clear family comes first. I will remember him for his kind words and support.

Angela, you know me, I could go on and on. These were special men. Being a woman in a male-dominated career was a learning experience and sometimes challenging. Looking back, I greatly enjoyed the company of those who've journeyed by my side.

What's a Heaven For?

My favorite saying is from poet Robert Browning:

> Ah, but a man's reach should exceed his grasp,
> Or what's a heaven for?

That striving, that desire, is so human. I would recommend to others a policing career. Our world is changing quickly and it needs good officers, good officers who are also good people, especially in today's world. It's always been a dangerous job but in modern times, it's getting worse; it's not just the bad guys we're fighting now. My son advised me recently not to advertise that I'm a retired cop. He said, "Mom, it's not safe." And he's not wrong.

Life for me after my service with the force is at times difficult. I live with anxiety and worry. My body is damaged. I can no longer defend myself. I can no longer run, yell, see or hear well. Most nights for me mean nightmares. Loud noises and bright lights hurt. When I hear a car backfire,

I hit the deck. Many cases and investigations have stayed with me. They still haunt me. I think about the victims and wonder if I could have done more to help them. I wonder how they are today. I wish the public realized the sacrifice police officers and their families make. Most people experience one or two traumatic events; we experience them routinely. It takes its toll. If we survive, we pay with our spirit, on and off the job and long into retirement ... forever. Our families pay, too.

I am not alone in my struggles post-service; many officers live with PTSD and some pay with their lives. There's a plaque outside of our Police Association office that lists the names of our members, dates hired, dates retired, and dates they died. The average is a five-year survival rate, post retirement. Some never get the opportunity to collect their first pension cheque, like Shawn and Teddy. We all carry trauma. Many suffer from PTSD. Some lose their families. Some, their lives.

A final note to Angela Keara, my great-great-granddaughter,

Now that you've read about my story and my ups and downs, I have a question I wish you could answer for me here in 2020: Would you ever join the police force? Many of my fellow officers look back on their history to find generations of those who became military, firemen, or police officers. A good book to read for historical information on Ottawa police officers, that helps keep my story alive is The History of the Ottawa Police, 1826 to 1993, *by Sgt. Gilles M. Larochelle. If you turn to page 316 in that book, you'll find my name, Trish Haley.*

Postscript to Trish Haley's story, Adventures on D Platoon

Marc Denis

■ ■ ■

CONSTABLE DAVID KIRKWOOD had been with the Ottawa Police Force for all of four months when he was killed. I never met the man. I was 15 years old, enjoying my summer holidays from school in the summer of 1977, living in the very blue-collar area of Mechanicsville. The incident happened less than five minutes from our house.

It was around 9 p.m. on July 11 when David Kirkwood and his coach officer were asked by two detectives to assist them as they attended a house on Gladstone Avenue to execute an arrest warrant — for assault causing bodily harm, on the 22-year-old son of the homeowners. While his coach officer went to the front door with one of the detectives, Kirkwood went to the rear of the house with the other. Within moments Kirkwood and one of the other officers were shot from an upstairs window. The other officer would survive, David Kirkwood would not. In the ensuing three-hour standoff, several other officers were injured and the house was in flames before the gunman, Frederick Koepke, surrendered, unhurt.

David Kirkwood was 21 years old when he was killed, and his young wife was expecting their first child. I never met David Kirkwood, but I met the man who killed him.

By the early 1990s, I was myself an Ottawa Police officer

working patrol in the downtown core, having been hired in October 1988. I can look back now and realize just how naive I was in my early days, and how the job was an eye-opener, maturing me quickly. I was working in one of six two-officer units, partnered with Joe Ieradi. "Big" Joe may have been a couple of inches shorter than my 6 feet, but he tipped the scales at a muscular 230, around 10 pounds more than me. Joe and I joined at the same time, and had been platoon mates since day one.

I think every police officer knows the feeling of hearing a call broadcast or a name checked over the radio that immediately brings you to attention, and spikes the adrenaline. One such call for me was in the early 1990s. A rookie officer in our patrol zone, Trish Haley, had stopped a vehicle on Cambridge Street, and, as was our habit, Joe and I started toward her location to drive by. This was normal safety procedure with any officer, to let them know help was close if needed, and to let the motorist know the officer who stopped them was not alone. Trish was new to the job, and although she still had a lot to learn, she was keen and wasn't afraid to work hard. My adrenaline spiked when she broadcast the name of the motorist she had stopped, Fred Koepke, and it went through the roof when she advised, stress in her voice, that he was being aggressive with her. We had dealt with Koepke before.

One evening on patrol, just a few weeks before, Joe and I responded to a complaint of yelling and screaming, the voices sounding like a man and a woman. We rolled up to the scene and could see two people, a man and a woman, arguing in the middle of the street. As we approached them, we told them to step away from each other, standard practice in cases like this, designed to allow us to speak to them separately. The man spoke up telling us to leave them alone, that they hadn't done anything, they hadn't called us — fairly typical behaviour in these cases. I pointed to the sidewalk and told him, firmly, to get to it. He did. Joe spoke with the woman on the opposite sidewalk. The man, much quieter now and sitting on the curb, told me that the woman was his girlfriend and they had been arguing. He denied there had been any assault by either one of them, and there were no obvious signs that there had been. When I asked for identification, he said that he didn't have his driver's licence, but he had the registration for the truck he owned. I told him that would do, and I very distinctly remember him handing it up to me from his seat on the curb and saying, "I'm pretty well-known around here." I read the name on the registration — Frederick Koepke.

I think every police officer knows the feeling of hearing a call broadcast or a name checked over the radio that immediately brings you to attention, and spikes the adrenaline.

Of course, I knew the name. After killing David Kirkwood, Koepke was found not guilty for reason of insanity, despite there being evidence at trial that he would lie to avoid responsibility for actions. He was sent away to an institution for the mentally ill. He spent ten years there, and eventually returned to Ottawa, to live with his parents, in the same house on Gladstone Avenue.

Only a few weeks before our encounter with him, our platoon had been advised that since his release, Koepke had been convicted of assaulting his mother, assaulting his girlfriend, and being in possession of drugs, and that he had also made an attempt to legally purchase an assault rifle, unsuccessfully. We were advised, of course, to use caution if we encountered him. I remember thinking, this guy sounds dangerous.

I checked Koepke's name but there were no warrants and no release conditions that he was breaching at the time. Joe and I conferred and, although the two had been arguing, there were no grounds to arrest either of them.

I looked down at Koepke and had a difficult time imagining that this person could inspire fear, or awe, or respect. He was short, gaunt, balding, dishevelled, and had the look of a drug user. This was a man who would assault his own mother. He seemed singularly unimpressive, and here he was being boastful about being "well-known around here." Well-known for killing a man with whom I likely would have worked one day.

Before sending him on his way, I asked Koepke what he meant by telling me he was well-known. He merely shrugged. I asked if he was proud of what he had done, whether he went around bragging about it, and did he try to impress his friends? He stammered a bit, and said he didn't mean anything by it. All the bravado was gone. I told him not to go around bragging about what he had done, that it was nothing to be proud of. I asked him too, if he went around bragging about beating up his mother. He just shrugged. I never raised my voice, and I didn't lose my cool. I would never want to give him the satisfaction. I wanted to appear bored by him, and unimpressed.

This was the first time I had ever dealt with Koepke, and I'm not sure what I expected him to be like, perhaps more imposing, more assured, more dangerous. He was none of these, but neither was he contrite, remorseful, embarrassed. He had started by playing the tough guy when we drove up, and ended up sitting meekly on the curb.

As Joe and I raced to Trish's location listening for updates, we heard other officers announce they were also attending, I was running the possible scenarios through my mind. I didn't think much of Koepke, but could he be drunk, on drugs, somehow out of control? It also occurred to me that Trish had stopped him literally around the corner from the house where he had killed David Kirkwood in 1977. I was ready for anything, and I knew Joe was too, although neither of us said a word. As I pulled the cruiser southbound onto Cambridge, I could see Koepke, in the street, by the door of Trish's cruiser, which faced northbound. I stopped a few meters away and Joe and I quickly stepped out. I remember Koepke's face turning towards us and our eyes met. I gestured him away from the cruiser, as I had done the first time we met, and he immediately stepped away from Trish, put his head down, and said to me, "Sorry officer," and words to the effect that he was only kidding around, and didn't mean anything by it. He stood where he was told, and was quiet and compliant from that point on. I couldn't help but think about how cheap he seemed. This tough guy, this cop-killer, this woman-beater — sounds dangerous on paper, but he was nothing more than a loud-mouth bully.

I can't even recall now how the rest of the call unfolded, other than there was nothing remarkable about it, my memory focused on Koepke's behaviour, and the very sad fact that someone like him could have actually taken the life of a man much better than him.

Over 25 years passed before I realized the impact the traffic stop had on Trish. We had, of course checked on her that evening, asking if she was alright, if there were grounds for an arrest, asking what she needed from us to help with the call, but she seemed fine, in complete control, and ready to finish the call, and the rest of the shift. She never let it be known, to me at least, that she was anything but fine. We worked closely for several years after that, part of a close-knit platoon of officers who worked hard, bounced ideas off each other, socialized, and laughed a lot.

As the years pass and I get together with officers with whom I've worked over the years, it becomes obvious that most of us remember calls and incidents differently, each having seemingly taken away something different. My takeaway from Trish's traffic stop was certainty different than hers. I came to learn of the stress, anxiety, and fear she felt. I wish I had known at the time. Joe and I had just enough time on the job to feel confident in dealing with most calls, and most people, not to mention being two big, strong men. Koepke had shown over the years that he had no respect for women (convicted in 2009 for criminal harassment for stalking a woman from his neighbourhood). Trish was fairly new on the job at the time she stopped him, and I believe that if the same thing had happened a couple of years later, it would have been a different experience for her.

Jackie Gordon is the Sergeant-at-Arms (SAA), the Executive Director of Precinct Properties and the Legislative Protective Service for the Legislative Assembly of Ontario. Jackie is the first female SAA in the Province of Ontario and the first full time female SAA in Canada. Prior to becoming SAA, Jackie was a member of the Halton Regional Police Service for 34+ years. She served in a supervisory or management role for the majority of her career in most areas of the policing. Jackie is the recipient of the Queen's Diamond Jubilee Medal for her community service and the Police Exemplary Medal for her career in policing service. She has been married for 38 years and is a proud mother of a talented, hardworking and intelligent daughter.

13

A JOURNEY TO BECOME THE FIRST FEMALE SERGEANT-AT-ARMS IN ONTARIO

■■■

Jackie Gordon

POLICING WAS A GOAL OF MINE from my early teenage years. As a woman working in a male-dominated profession, I recognized from the onset that this decision would be fraught with challenges. I was determined, hardworking, compassionate, and resilient, and these qualities were key in helping me navigate these uncharted waters. I also had a genuine desire to serve my community, and I believed wholeheartedly that the actions of one person could make the community, and our world, a better place to live. My 34-year policing career was built on these values that would eventually lead me to an opportunity to change history by becoming the first female Sergeant-at-Arms (SAA) in Ontario and the first full-time female SAA in Canada.

If you were to ask me what aspect of my policing had the greatest influence on my career, I would have to identify my assignment as a foot patrol officer in a high density, low-income area in Burlington, Ontario, a city located at the head of Lake Ontario, 50 km west of Toronto.

I was selected by the 3 District Inspector of the Halton Regional Police Service, along with four male officers, to work exclusively in this one-square-mile community for a period of six months. Significant police resources were being consumed by the needs of this community and our job was to reduce the crime rate. Some of the local tenants were very hostile towards the police — we never left our cruisers unattended at calls in this neighbourhood due to risk of damage.

The underlying problems in this community involved many complex social issues. This assignment would require us to dig deeper into the community to understand the problems and find solutions. Traditional policing efforts had failed and this assignment would afford us the opportunity to implement some unconventional methods to address the underlying causes and win the support of law-abiding families who were living there in fear. It also allowed me to look inward and examine my own personal bias. I recognized that I had preconceived notions of this rundown neighbourhood and the people who lived there.

Community Facelift
Our first response was to address appearance of the Burlington area by giving the neighbourhood a facelift. It was run down and 'slum' landlords did very little to keep the buildings clean or clear of clutter. This neighbourhood had a poor reputation and many residents living in the community were ashamed to admit they were from this area.

The strategy was that our team would stay for six months and spend considerable time building relationships and working on each issue we identified as being contributors to the crime rate. I developed relationships with this community that enabled us, as police, to arrest and charge drug dealers and criminals from the housing complexes and successfully evict them. The quality of life for the families steadily improved, trust was established, and the relationship grew between local residents and police. The crime rate began to drop steadily which meant our policing approach was working. However, during our impending departure, residents expressed genuine fear that things would return to the old normal after we left. I offered to stay behind and patrol because I felt there was more to accomplish. We had only scratched the surface, and I wanted to get to the social issues that would ultimately create a healthy, safe environment for local residents.

During that year, I strengthened the residents' relationship with the police and gave them a political voice. I identified underlying causes for some of their issues and felt this needed a coordinated approach of services if we were to make any permanent impact. I witnessed the cycle of poverty that I believed could be broken for the next generation if they had better coordination of services and more opportunities. I brought together all the community partners and government who were spending millions of dollars providing the local residents with services. I decided to host a meeting so that each community partner could share what services they were providing and the cost to support local residents with these services. It was obvious what was required to change in order to sustain the improvements.

One of the initiatives I decided to implement was a summer day camp, and invited the Region of Halton — Children Services to participate in order to support disadvantaged children from the area. We used this time to introduce positive role models into their lives and used the time to work on self-esteem, self-care and the law. We took these local children on day trips such as the zoo in order to gain experiences outside of their community. This was a first for many children because their neighbourhood was only place they knew.

During the course of that summer, the crime rate had plummeted and vandalism was negligible. This program provided the evidence necessary to identify a genuine need for resources in the community and it made me determined to ensure it would and could be sustained without the police, that is with the right social supports. I worked closely with the local politicians at all levels of government to discuss ways to assist with community needs.

Before leaving this community, I had secured the support of CAS and the Regional Health and Children Services department to host a 'mom and tot' program in the community, which became the grassroots model upon which the foundation for the Early Years Centers in Ontario was built. The community received funding from the City of Burlington for a playground and basketball courts, and a local not-for-profit organization held an after-school program that included tutoring and recreational activities. The following year, the city held a summer camp that continues to be offered yearly. Services also became integrated and better coordinated, but most importantly, sustainable. The community underwent a transformation and residents began to feel a sense of pride. These changes were the work of many people including fellow officers. I do not take credit for all of these achievements as it was the combined hard work of many people, but I take pride on how we successfully mobilized this community into action.

I left this assignment with a greater appreciation for the challenges of youth, a better understanding of the cycle of poverty and the privilege of getting to know the many amazing and courageous people who called this community home — the same people I had harshly judged when I first arrived. I worked hard to give them a voice when no one was listening. This position challenged my thinking on the traditional role of police and whether arresting criminals and giving out the tickets was truly effective without addressing the real underlying issues. I recognized early in my career that I could help the underserved and learn from my community and, in the process, I learned a lot about myself. The only way I could do my job in a meaningful way was to educate myself about the places in which I served, and to work alongside the people to make their neighbourhoods safe places to live, work and play.

This was a pinnacle point in my career, and it shaped the person and officer I became. I dedicated many off-duty hours helping the underserved throughout my career. I focused my energy on three groups that I believed needed the support and leadership of the police. These included youth, persons suffering from mental illnesses, and persons from different cultures and religions who needed educational opportunities in order to promote respect and acceptance.

My journey in policing was very enjoyable but obviously very challenging. Most of the challenges in my policing career came from the discrimination I experienced as a woman and in my latter career, the brass ceiling, a police version of the glass ceiling. The community recognized my potential as a future senior leader (chief), however the senior management of my police service did not. My approach to policing was anything but traditional. I cared about people and I did not allow policing to change that in me. It was my True North.

More Courage to Try
I felt I had more to offer in terms of leadership and the status quo was not an option. I saw the direction of the Service as regressive and I was no longer challenged. Although disappointed that I was unable to reach the goal of leading a police service, I was grateful for all the opportunities my policing career afforded me. I recognized I had more to learn, more to give and the courage to try. No one had control of my destiny but me. My determination, resiliency, and effort would ultimately be the key to my success.

The year I departed, I received the formal recognition of the Queen Elizabeth's Diamond Jubilee medal for serving on more than thirty-five boards and committees. Throughout my career, I became adept at navigating the politics and bureaucracy to address the needs of the underserved and disadvantaged. Leadership came easy and the ability to form lasting relationships proved essential in helping my community address underlying causes of crime. It was time for me go. Ironically, my teenage daughter Holly and I were both at crossroads where we needed to decide what we wanted to do with our lives. It was a big world out there and the possibilities were endless.

Sergeant-at-Arms
The next stop in my career was a brief one. I spent the next eighteen months working for the Ministry of Education developing emergency management policies for the Ontario provincial schools for the Deaf and Blind. This opportunity reinforced the importance of establishing relationships. When I came to work, I quickly recognized that the School for the Blind was not meeting the Fire Code. The relationship with the fire department was non-existent. Furthermore, the building staff failed to address outstanding Fire Code violations adequately. In order to address these issues, I decided to educate myself on fire safety. I enrolled in night school to learn about Fire Inspections. As a result, I addressed the outstanding concerns in partnership with the fire department and school staff. These efforts improved the safety of the children, school, and established a working, functional relationship with the fire department. I also wrote and installed emergency packages with complete instructions on what to do in different types of emergencies in every room in all the schools.

The rest, I guess you can say is history. I have spent the past four years in the role of Sergeant-at-Arms and Executive Director of Precinct Properties. It has been a demanding and challenging role, but a rewarding one. All of the skills and knowledge in my policing career have been utilized. With the support of dedicated staff and the leadership of a progressive Clerk and Speaker, efforts to improve the safety and security at the Ontario Legislative Precinct has been evolving rapidly. Additionally, significant effort has gone into modernizing the Legislative Protective Service.

The experiences of my policing career have taught me the importance of determination, hard work, resiliency, and the importance of establishing good relationships in order to achieve success. It has shown me that self-reflection and self-awareness towards your biases is essential in being a successful leader. I am grateful that I have been able to elevate the presence of women in one of the several remaining male bastions. My picture now hangs in the hallway of the Ontario Legislature alongside many other 'remarkable women' of Parliament. It continues to be an honour to represent women at the Ontario Legislative Assembly and to lead the Legislative Protective Service and the Legislative Assembly forward in making several historical changes in public safety and security.

Ron Pond is a former member of the RCMP originally from Fredericton, New Brunswick. One homicide case was featured in a book Life with Billy and a television movie. The UFO sighting has been featured in several publications including Dark Object and numerous airings on the TV series Sightings. He is an award-winning community leader, volunteer and activist. He and wife Jo have lived north of the 60th parallel for close to fifty years in communities from the Eastern Arctic to Yukon. They also enjoyed many years in Nova Scotia. Ron and his family currently reside in Whitehorse, Yukon.

14

THEFT OF *THE CAPE SPRY* AND OTHER INVESTIGATIONS

■■■

Ron Pond

I GREATLY ENJOYED my twenty-three years of service in the RCMP and have nothing but respect for the men and women whom I had the opportunity to work with. Much of my career was spent in the Northwest Territories, in charge of the Yellowknife Drug Section and in Yarmouth General Investigation Section (GIS), which was responsible for assisting all Southern Nova Scotia detachments in serious investigations. While still a member, organizing events and activities increased my interaction with the general public and led to my current involvement with volunteering and social issues.

My life after the force is linked in many ways to overall investigative case experiences in Nova Scotia and Northwest Territories but not directly to any one particular file. In this chapter I relate a number of these stories from small communities where I served. They have all informed my decision to concentrate on volunteer work in my retirement — volunteering really defines who I have become.

Nova Scotia, Clever Thievery on the Cape Spry
In the summer of 1966, I was a member of "O" Troop, one of the last RCMP troops that happened to have full

horsemanship training. It was from O Troop that I graduated into my life as an member of the RCMP. After a brief posting to New Minas, Nova Scotia, I was posted to the small town of Barrington Passage.

The first of several interesting incidents I was involved in was the theft of a 100-foot dragger, the Cape Spry from Lockport Harbour in southeastern Nova Scotia. This is a story of clever thievery that didn't work out, but then it did.

---

*I was ordered to jump from the
Coast Guard boat to the Cape Spry to make the arrest.
If I mistimed the jump, I would be lost
forever in the deep and dark ocean.*

Early Friday morning on the 17th of March, 1967 a fisherman skillfully navigated alone out of the perilous Lockport Harbour in the Cape Spry, a scallop dragger that normally required a crew of three to five men. He accomplished this solo navigation by going back and forth from the below deck engine room to the controls located on the main deck level. Things were going well for him on this journey until about 250 miles south of Lockport when the Cape Spry started taking on water, forcing him to call for assistance.

A Corporal and I boarded a Coast Guard ship at Shelbourne on Saturday and began our pursuit south on a stormy and windy Atlantic Ocean. I was seasick from the time our ship left dock. Sometime after midnight on Sunday we caught up to the Cape Spry in the dark and stormy ocean and maneuvered beside her. The two ships would momentarily crash together and, as junior member, I was ordered to jump from the Coast Guard boat to the Cape Spry to make the arrest. If I mistimed the jump, I would be lost forever in the deep and dark ocean. Both ships were now covered in thick ice. Needless to say, I successfully jumped onto the Cape Spry and subsequently repeated the effort back to the Coast Guard ship, accompanied by my prisoner. After a crew of Coast Guard sailors were deployed to the Cape Spry, we returned to Shelbourne, arriving on Monday. Over the entire return trip, I played cribbage with the prisoner and got to know him. He was a decent individual who, after over indulging in alcohol, made a mistake that would cost him some jail time. Things worked out for him in the end — as he was being sentenced in court, the owner of the Cape Spry hired him to go to work for him when released.

Dare I mention again that I was seasick the entire voyage back, cribbage game and all? That was the end of my sailing career.

The UFO Sighting at Shag Harbour
Another significant incident was the UFO sighting at Shag Harbour, Nova Scotia on October 4th, 1967. To this day the sighting remains one of the most reported-on and investigated UFO sightings in Canadian history and is also the world's only government-documented UFO crash. Reports and investigations were conducted by the RCMP, Canadian Coast Guard, Canadian Forces Navy and Air Force, and the US Condon Committee, which is the informal name of the University of Colorado UFO Project, a group funded by the United States Air Force to study unidentified flying objects

Shortly before midnight on October 4th, 1967 I, along with two other members of the RCMP, responded to the report of an airplane crash at Shag Harbour. I was left on shore to observe and take notes while the other two members secured a boat to investigate the incident. After being searched by teams of divers, nothing was ever found at the scene or on the ocean bed. Numerous reliable witnesses from as far away as Halifax up the eastern coast of Nova Scotia reported for a week about this sighting and related sightings The night of the incident, all I was witness to was a single light in the middle of Shag Harbour which, over a short period of time, moved out of the harbour against the tide leaving a strip of foamed water about a mile in length.

A picnic ground and UFO Gazebo are currently located at Shag Harbour overlooking the site. Laurie Wickens, who initially reported this incident, currently runs a museum in Barrington, Nova Scotia focused on the UFO sighting. I was interviewed on camera by Universal Studios for the ongoing TV series, *Sightings* with my interview being aired many times.

A Precious Cargo
In the early 80s the late Bill Parker, one of the best policemen I have had the pleasure of working with, a great friend and a pretty fair heart card player, was the lead investigator on a drug case I assisted with. Information had been provided that a ship containing a cargo of marijuana was destined for the rugged south shore of Nova Scotia. This was followed up with an investigation for an extended period of time. The ship eventually arrived and its illegal cargo was unloaded by the crew and a number of locals where it was distributed to three locations. I was tasked to lead one of the three teams assigned to conduct a search, arrest anyone found on the premises and to secure any contraband found at that location. My target was a small bungalow where we did, in fact, seize bailed and wrapped marijuana that at that time was worth a street value of eleven million dollars ($11,000,000!). The total seizure from the three locations searched that day was estimated to be twenty-three million

dollars ($23,000,000!). Not a bad day and I certainly appreciated being part of this case.

A Couple of Homicide Investigations
While in charge of the General Investigation Section in Yarmouth, Nova Scotia, I was the main support investigator for two homicide cases. The first one was when Billy Stafford was murdered by his wife as his slept behind the steering wheel of his truck. The case led to the writing and publication of two true-crime books and a made-for-TV movie.

Another Nova Scotia case that had an interesting aspect to it was a homicide I worked in Yarmouth in the early 1980s. Two young girls along with their father had arrived back in Ontario after a summer holiday at their cabin in Nova Scotia, but without the mother or the 16-year-old brother Reacting to concern from relatives, the summer cabin retreat was checked out. To give some perspective to the scene, the house, a weathered, unpainted house located on the shore of a bay, was found clouded in fog with every window and door boarded up — a scene you would likely be familiar with from many mystery-horror films. Other than to say that the mutilated body of the mother was found in a second-floor bedroom and the body of the 16-year-old brother was found on the living/kitchen room floor, I will not describe the grisly scene we found inside.

Along with another RCMP officer, I subsequently travelled to St. Catharines, Ontario where we sat down with the father, who was the prime suspect in the murder. His lawyer was also present. After being given a standard police caution, the father gave us a lengthy confession, signing each page to signify the voluntary nature of the statement. His lawyer then signed alongside of each of his client's signatures to further signify the voluntary statement. I then produced a Polaroid photograph of what we believed to be the weapon used in this crime, a two-foot bait knife. Both the suspect and his lawyer then signed the back of the photograph to confirm that this was indeed the weapon used.

Several months later we subpoenaed the client's lawyer to testify at the voir dire hearing at the trial to determine the admissibility of the statement and identification of the weapon. The statement and identification were accepted, which was of great value in convicting the father, landing him 25 years behind bars. Needless to say, his legal colleagues were none too pleased with the actions of this lawyer.

Treating People Right
A robbery with violence, emphasized for me how you treat people involved in investigations — in this case, the suspects. An elderly gentleman, the owner and sole staff in a small grocery and coffee business, was found unconscious on the floor of his establishment in the south end of Yarmouth. In that he remained unconscious for several days — there were no visible signs of any struggle and no way to verify if anything was missing — it was assumed by those first on the scene that he had fallen off a stool. Digging around however, I was able to locate a taxi driver who had driven two rather suspicious individuals from the same area around the same time to a tavern in Halifax, a distance of approximately 300 kilometres. On a hunch, totally without any evidence and with having received no complaint, I drove to Halifax with another member. We located two individuals in a tavern who fit the description I had been given. We arrested the two brothers and returned to Yarmouth where they provided me with written confessions to having robbed and assaulted the owner of the shop. They thanked me for the way they had been treated and shook my hand before they were sentenced each to fifteen years.

Northwest Territories

I transferred to the Northwest Territories in the fall of 1967 where I was stationed in several small communities, in charge of the Yellowknife Drug Section. It was in these small communities where the First Nations and Inuit Peoples comprised a significant portion of the population. All nature of alcohol-related incidents were reported and investigated on a regular basis, in addition to small break enters and thefts into businesses. Truth be known is that despite the high number of alcohol-related incidents, the vast majority of the community did not cross our path in the course of duties. The majority of people were law abiding and alcohol was not a major part of their lives.

The Crash of a Beechcraft

An incident of interest was the crash of a Beechcraft south of Frobisher Bay, NWT (now Iqaluit, Nunavut). The airplane owned by Coleman Aircraft Industry was being ferried from Chicago to England by three pilots when it crashed into the top of a mountain killing all three on board. I was assigned responsibility for going to the scene to conduct the initial investigation and to secure the scene for a Ministry of Transport (MOT) Investigator. I was accompanied to the scene by an RCMP Special Constable and two Canadian Armed Forces members. We were flown by an RCMP Twin Otter to a location a few kilometres from the base of the mountain and the location of the crash.

Upon landing, we had to quickly unload our gear, including two Skidoos, because the aircraft was slowly breaking through the ice on the creek on which it had landed. The temperature including wind chill was approaching -80 F degrees and the sky was clear, with little wind. As the aircraft safely departed, we loaded our gear on wooden sleds and made our way to the base of the mountain where the military had set up their camp, including the erection of a floorless bell tent. At that moment, we discovered that the snow knife to build an igloo had been left behind, as had the fuel for the stove. It was a tough moment because having built igloos, I can attest to their comfort, that, when built efficiently, maintain a temperature of about 50 F degrees. Much better than the military's floorless bell tent.

It was impossible to radio for supplies to be dropped off as our radios had already frozen in the extreme cold temperature. The Special and I made our way to the top of the mountain to examine the crash site. It was evident that the aircraft had flown straight into the mountain and the bodies of the three pilots were quickly found and identified. When I began drawing a rough sketch of the scene and making notes, I had to use a pencil because the pens had frozen, and the paper froze and broke. We made our way back to the campsite when we had completed all that we could in the extreme cold. We sat with the military chaps in the tent that they had erected, the only source of light and heat being a small heater the military provided.

Trying to eat sandwiches we had brought with us that had now turned to, basically, ice cubes presented quite a challenge. Likewise, tea froze as quickly as it was brewed requiring us to warm the mugs with our warm hands long enough to get a sip at a time. We spent the night in our sleeping bags awake and chattering in the cold, no doubt near hyperthermia. The next morning while the soldiers broke camp, the Special and I made our way back up to the top of the mountain where we stacked the three bodies on a sled. They were so frozen by this time that when we tapped on them, their bodies sounded like hollow plastic. We then made our way down to the campsite and then up a grade to a plateau perhaps two kilometres to the west. We determined that this place would make a good landing site for the RCMP Twin Otter instead of the creek where the aircraft had almost broken through. The Special drove the Skidoo while I followed on foot through waist-deep snow, occasionally straightening the ever-shifting stack of bodies. The soldiers followed with their Skidoo and all the gear from the campsite.

Despite the cold temperature, this journey completed under the intense arctic sun was quite agreeable. It wasn't very long after we got there that the RCMP Twin Otter landed. The gear and bodies were loaded while the MOT Investigator quickly made his way to the crash site and returned just as quickly, having completed what he was required to do. We then returned to Frobisher Bay where we welcomed warm shelter.

Trapped in an Igloo
Another rather humorous incident, that I have recounted many times involving an igloo occurred when I was building one with another member as part of a survival course. We had completed the construction of the igloo and both of us had to change our undergarments due to being quite wet with sweat. I was inside the igloo up on the raised sleeping platform hanging our wet garments on a line we had strung for that purpose. By now, the igloo was quite structurally sound. A small sardine can filled with oil was lit to serve the purpose of our heat and light. The flame was larger than we had planned, and before I could stop him, my partner entered the igloo and threw water on the burning oil creating a larger fire that threatening to engulf the drying clothes in flames. I was basically trapped. Can you imagine if the flames had been sufficient to cause my demise what the obituary would read like?

Roads and Animals
Mid-winter in the late 1960s, a trapper's body was found deceased in his cabin in the wilderness outside of Fort Smith, NWT. I drove the deceased from Fort Smith to Hay River where I observed his autopsy. My vehicle was an older

panel truck with no heat, insulation, or any extras currently standard on any vehicle. In the early morning hours after the autopsy I drove the deceased back to Fort Smith. I encountered no traffic either way on this 170-mile gravel highway which at the time was basically wilderness. About halfway back on the return trip, I stopped to close my eyes for a few moments. When I awoke, the truck was totally surrounded by about a dozen wolves, all sitting on their haunches, no doubt smelling the deceased. I attempted to roll down the window to better take in the scene when in an instance they disappeared, not to be seen again.

Later in the summertime just outside of Fort Smith on the same road, I was riding my motorcycle and I came upon a large herd of wood bison just off the roadway. As I approached, they started to cross the road, forcing me to stop. As these slow-moving rather large and majestic animals crossed the road, they totally enveloped me and my motorcycle. At any point I could have reached out and touched them in any direction. At any point of course they could have crushed me and the motorcycle. Gratefully, they perceived that I was no threat.

Hostage Negotiation
A decision I made early in my career was to talk my way out of situations instead of fighting. Having had several physical encounters, I felt it only a matter of time before someone got the best of me and I certainly had to do everything within my means to not let that happen. The more I took this approach, the more accomplished I got at reducing physical altercations, improving my negotiating skills and interviewing skills.

I was eventually trained as a 'Hostage Negotiator' and was recognized for my interviewing skills. Taking this approach also showed me that the majority of individuals we were investigating were, for the most part, good individuals that had made a mistake. This might have been due to addictions (alcohol or drugs), a crime of passion or domestic situation, outside influence or peer pressure just to name a few of the stimuli that cause people to take the wrong path. I found that a talking rather than a fighting approach also greatly reduced the feeling of hostility by those I encountered.

Volunteering in Yukon
As I have said before, volunteering clearly defines who I am. My volunteer work in the community started in earnest shortly after moving to the Yukon in 1983, while I was still a member of the Force. I joined a local Lions Club and over the period of a year, I organized a Lions International drug awareness program targeting mid to older schoolchildren. This program, which involved training over 75 teachers from the Yukon and Alaska, was implemented into the curriculum of the Yukon and Alaska schools. I then expanded on this by introducing another drug awareness program into the Yukon targeting younger kids and involving a mascot that became very popular with all ages in the years to follow.

Over the years, I have introduced seven mascots to the Yukon in connection with other organizations. This initiative was quite instrumental in my foray into the volunteer world. I met many great people, learned new skills, and also provided a way for people to interact with a police officer in a positive way. If I may quote Mr. Sam Rivera, President of the Fortune Society in New York, a society that has been helping people cope with life after incarceration; "The crime is what you did. The crime is not who you are." Volunteering enabled me to confirm that many if not the majority of individuals I crossed paths with as a member of the RCMP were decent people, who, for one reason or another, had made mistakes in their lives.

While still a member of the Force, I was on the executive for several curling associations. I bid on and acted as Host Chairman organizing the National Police Curling Championship in Whitehorse in 1987 and also hosted another National Police Curling championship a few years later. While still a member, I initiated the process to form a Yukon Division of the RCMP Veterans Association which is still active and which I served in all Executive positions for a number of years. I also served on the National Executive for the Veterans Association for a number of years. I have since been bestowed with the honour of 'Life Membership' in both organizations in recognition of my efforts. Since retiring, I have also acted as Host Chair for two National RCMP Veteran's Association Annual General Meetings in Whitehorse.

In the years to follow, I have served on, or with, in excess of three dozen organizations, events, and causes, primarily in the role of President or Chair or in another executive position at the Yukon, National and International level. It has been an extremely rewarding effort where the benefits far exceeded any efforts I have made. With some of the activities, I have enjoyed the ability to work with people with mental health issues and addictions and who are down on their luck for various reasons, homeless or otherwise.

For a dozen years I volunteered with an awesome group of volunteers from my Church and the community in general in organizing a Sunday meal for this targeted group. We personally paid all the costs to provide a full meal including all the trimmings that any one of us would have been proud to have served in our own homes. In addition, we provided a takeaway snack. It was during these meals that many of those attending would approach me, not only expressing their appreciation, but to tell me a bit about their lives and how they got to where they were at the time.

While with the Church, I took a year-long course to

become a licensed lay minister. A professor, who had just returned from Israel and Palestine with the World Council of Churches as an Ecumenical Accompaniers for Peace in Palestine and Israel (EAPPI, EA), came up from Edmonton. I became interested and took up an opportunity to volunteer in a role that would offer opportunities to work with both Israelis and Palestinians in a positive role. I successfully went through the lengthy indoctrination and training, some of it in Switzerland, and eventually spent three months in the southern Hebron Hill of Palestine as a non-violent observer of Human Rights issues and Humanitarian issues. This indeed was an eye-opening experience, sometimes tense, but the nevertheless a great opportunity to work with volunteers from around the globe and to witness people living under very difficult circumstances.

The Yukon Anniversaries Commission and MMRC

My volunteer efforts while in the RCMP were instrumental in my success in securing a position with the Yukon Anniversaries Commission. I was still serving as the RCMP Division Staff Relations Representative when, in October of 1988, I successfully applied for the position as Executive Director for the Yukon Anniversaries Commission. It was established to work with the Yukon communities and representatives initially from Alaska, British Columbia, Alberta, and the Northwest Territories. I was to organize, coordinate and promote activities commemorating the 50th Anniversary of the construction of the Alaska Highway in 1992 and the 100th anniversary of the Klondike Gold Rush in 1998.

Then in 1995, I accepted the position as General Manager for Mount McIntyre Recreation Centre (MMRC). This facility was initially built in 1980 to host the World Cup for Cross County Skiing. In 1986, a world-class eight-sheet curling facility was added to the initial structure.

MMRC boasted over 70 kilometres of ski trails, many of them lighted. During my tenure as manager, we hosted many events and banquets for up 1,500 attendees.

In 2000 I started driving school bus on the belief that the job would provide me the flexibility I needed to stay on top of the ever-increasing volunteer commitments I was making. This didn't work out. I retired totally from working in 2011 to concentrate on my work as a volunteer.

To be Recognized, or Not?
I have been recognized many times over the years for my volunteer efforts. I am most humbled and proud to have received the Governor General's Caring Canadian Award and subsequently the Sovereign's Medal for Volunteers, The Commissioner of the Yukon Annual Award for Public Service, Queen Elizabeth's Bi-Centennial Medal, and the Lions International Melvin Jones Award for Humanitarian Service. After receiving an enormous amount of recognition, I have spent the last number of years trying to maintain a low profile and submitting names of very deserving individuals for awards and recognition. I find this much more rewarding than actually receiving any more recognition.

This wasn't always the case. A few years into volunteering in Whitehorse I was feeling pretty good about myself if not smug about my volunteer efforts. I attended a function where the volunteer of the year for the City of Whitehorse was to be nominated, and I felt confident that I would receive this recognition. When I opened the door into the hall, I could see the room crowded with people whom I knew deserved the award more than myself. In fact, the award went very properly to a good friend who has since passed. This was a humbling experience that has stuck with me over all the years since. It goes without saying that my wife and family have been very supportive given the countless hours I wasn't present.

I have to attribute considerable credit to a very important group of mentors and friends from before my time in the Force for my strong social beliefs, my anti-bigotry, my anti-racism and my overall belief that everyone is equal regardless of religious beliefs, ethnicity, colour of one's skin or sexual beliefs. I am proud that I have been an influence on my children and grandchildren who also hold these same strong anti-racist beliefs. A group that I have been proudly associated with as a member is a small group of Scouters known as 'The Miramichi Pioneers.' As a group and individually, they have supported and mentored me since the mid-1950s. Even now, we meet via Zoom monthly and when possible we reunite for tales and tea on the banks of the Miramichi. With this organization I have been bestowed the name *Maugn Nyah Toh* and all of us have the authority to use the initials "MP" after our names.

Val Hoglund is a senior constable with the Edmonton Police Service. Val studied Physical Education at the University of Alberta, and General Studies at Ryerson University in Ontario. Val is a Certified Restorative Justice Facilitator, and is also an Equine-assisted Personal Development Coach. She has concentrated her 30-year career on helping children, youth, and families. The highlight of her career was when she was in Youth Unit and was partnered with a therapy dog. Val was the recipient of a provincial team award for her work in the Youth Unit.

15

IF YOU HELP ONE, THEY SAY YOU HELP SEVEN

■ ■ ■

Val Hoglund

POLICING is a uniquely diverse career. I have always said that policing is multiple careers, all in one. I have worked in every patrol division, and specialized areas such as: School Resource Officer Unit, Child at Risk Response Team, Human Resources Division, Recruiting Unit, Community Crime Management Team, Youth Unit, and I am now in the Human-centered Engagement Liaison Partnership Unit (HELP).

I learned the most, and changed as a person the most, when I worked with repeat offenders in Youth Unit. Upon acceptance into the Youth Unit, I had twenty-three years of service and I had raised two children of my own. I thought I knew a lot. Then I met a high-risk youth. I learned quickly that I was a high-risk cop. High risk to judge. High risk to shame. High risk to blame. High risk to be the stereotypical problem-solver, planner and dictator. High risk of being the exact version of the 'popo' the 'high-risk' youth called us.

Are any of those qualities in a cop actually helpful? After all, police candidates go into this line of work to help people. Aren't problem solvers valuable? I like to believe that I have a combination of book-smart and street-smart skills. Both are necessary to be an effective police officer.

But the one, and maybe only, skill I needed to work effectively with justice-involved youth was — listening.

Getting Out of Uniform
A wise social worker, who I was fortunate to have met early in my Youth Unit position, gave me some good advice, "Zip your lips, sit on your hands, open your ears and really listen. Listen for three hours if you have to." She was adamant about it. I recall, ignorantly thinking, how absurd it was for any professional to listen to anyone for three hours. I thought to myself it must be nice to have that kind of time. "It's all about the relationships," continued my astute social worker friend maintained. "It may take years to earn their trust," she said, making further ridiculous statements, in my opinion. By now I thought she was just as crazy as some of the kids on my caseload. I am a cop. It's my job to tell people to do the right thing when they are doing something wrong.

She continued, "You will see a striking change in their behaviour, especially toward authority, if you are lucky enough to earn their trust," she accurately predicted. Little did I know at the time, my work friend was describing social policing: building relationships with community members.

After my first year in Youth Unit, and ignoring the worthy advice that the discerning social worker had given me, I had only succeeded in getting the youth on my caseload to fear me and my uniform. They failed to show up at prearranged meetings and I had few positive interventions to report to my supervisor, even though I had good intentions. The social worker was right and I was wrong.

"I need to be out of uniform," I identified to my supervisor, "the kids don't trust me." I may as well have been wearing a 'Beware of Cop' sign around my neck. Surprisingly, he agreed with this suggestion, and, in plain clothes, I began doing proactive work with the law-breaking teens. It helped, a little. But only a little. I was still a cop with a gun on my hip, but at least I wasn't in full uniform anymore. It was my job to engage the teenagers and to reduce crime, but I was having a really hard time engaging with them. Earning their trust was going to take years.

Then, one magical day, something happened that would reshape the path of my career forever. Our squad was receiving a team award, and during the ceremony, I observed a corrections officer — along with her very handsome, furry, four-legged partner — receive an award for their proactive work with gang prevention in the Edmonton Remand Centre. My sergeant was sitting beside me and he keenly noticed my eyes were glued to the stage. Just as I was about to speak, he held up his hand, as if to physically block my words, while he overruled, "Don't even think about it, Hoglund. You're not getting a dog."

Oh, but I did think about it. I couldn't stop thinking about it. I didn't have a suitable dog at the time. I went home and looked at my three farm dogs: too hyper, too fat, too blind.

The Perfect Dog, Hershey

One year later, however, I finally did have the perfect dog: Hershey. After Hershey was approved to come to work with me, two things happened immediately. One, the youth forgot my name; only Hershey's name ever seemed important to them. Two, my phone never stopped ringing. "When is Hershey coming to see me?" the young animal lovers would plead.

Now let me tell you the story that made it all worthwhile. There were many, but there's always one that stands out.

Six years ago: meeting Amber

AMBER: Child >> Marginalized >> Orphaned >> Fostered >> Intelligent >> Sensitive >> Polite >> Adolescent >> Attractive >> Compounded loss >> Group home >> Naïve >> Hurt >> Angry >> Rebellious >> Addicted >> Gangs >> Drop-out >> Criminal >> Dangerous >> Lost >> Scared >>Hopeless >> Untrusting >> Alone >> Jailed

VAL: Child >> Privileged >> Suffered loss >> Adult >> Educated >> Enforcement >> Empathetic >> Diligent >>Experienced >> Judgmental >> Ignorant

I will never forget the first day I met Amber in 2015 (Amber is not her real name.) I was in Youth Unit and I had an office in Amber's junior high school. Her tragic history is almost identical to many wonderful Indigenous children and, sadly, includes many hardships. Amber was fourteen years old and in grade 9 when our paths crossed. This beautiful Indigenous girl had been up all night and came to school while high on drugs. She was wearing cannabis-printed leggings. I looked down at my therapy dog, Hershey (whom I'd been working with for about a year by then), as I said to him, "Boy, do we have our work cut out for us."

I bent down in front of Amber and showed her Hershey's best trick, something that usually makes teens, who are generally unsure about police, laugh. "Hide from the cops!" I said, and he lay down and covered his eyes with his paws. But this street-tough, stunning girl stiffly rolled her eyes and didn't even crack a smile.

I sighed and stood up straight. I asked Amber if she would like to come on a field trip with me. I was taking ten students over to the Northern Alberta Institute of Technology (NAIT), a polytechnical college. I was pleasantly surprised when she agreed to come. Maybe Hershey's trick wasn't so terrible after all. We walked the few blocks together as a group, with my handsome, furry partner who never has to shave by my side.

Once we arrived at NAIT, Amber told me she was interested in a career in culinary arts or mechanics. She wouldn't tell me much else. When we entered the kitchen, she pointed to some bacon, made an 'oink' sound and winked at me while smiling. I chuckled and thought how I was happy to be on the "let's tease the pig" wagon, rather than on no wagon with her at all.

After our tour of the kitchen and the mechanic shop, Amber disappeared — or 'jetted', in her words. Didn't even say goodbye. I was pleased, though, that she had given me the time she had. I hoped our next visit would be longer.

Little did I know at the time, I would eventually become Amber's mentor, and over the next six years of her life, we would grow incredibly close. Her to me, and, unexpectedly, me to her.

My interview with Amber, December 2020
Amber has a large family. Seven girls and two boys, or "Ten million," she proudly described, and it was the best part of her childhood.

When Amber was about five years old, she sorrowfully remembers being apprehended, along with two of her sisters, by Child and Family Services (CFS). Amber recalls they were sent to a city in British Columbia for a short period of time and later given back to their mother.

At the age of six, Amber was apprehended by CFS for the last time. Amber recalls the police had assisted on that apprehension. She had dropped some money her mother had given her and it had fallen under the police car. She hurtfully remembers the police officer not allowing her to pick it up.

She was placed in a foster home with her eldest sister by one year, but was split up from her only younger sister (and six older siblings). The foster family already had four foster children, and they only had room for two more. It was a devastating separation, of course.

The foster home, located in a suburb of Edmonton, was less than a welcoming environment. Amber described her foster family as deceiving, manipulative, and racist. Amber told me her foster mother spoke terribly of Amber's family, to Amber and her sister, declaring to the girls that her new foster parents were all they had.

Amber saw her mother on the curb waiting for the social worker to stop the car. Instead of stopping, the social worker told Amber that her mom hadn't shown up and then simply drove right past her.

Amber said, "Our foster parents used to make my sister and me feel ashamed about being Indigenous, even though our foster mother was Métis herself. From the location of our home, we could hear Poundmaker's Lodge, and our foster mother would make fun of them."

Amber referred to her foster mother as Evillene, the Wicked Witch of the West. Evillene forced Amber and her sister to completely lose touch with their older siblings. Losing bonds with her siblings was devastating to Amber. She loved being a part of a large family and, later in life, she had to rebuild her relationships with them, which hasn't been easy, but is important to Amber.

Although few, there were some positives about Amber's

foster home. When she was about eight years old, the foster family went on a road trip to Arizona and Nevada with Evillene's brother and his six foster children. Amber refers to these other children as her foster cousins, whom she enjoyed spending a lot of time with. She recalls it was a fun trip and she has good memories of that vacation.

Amber used to visit her biological mother once in a while, when she was permitted to do so. She recalled a specific scheduled visit in particular; while driving with a social worker to visit her mother, Amber saw her mother on the curb waiting for the social worker to stop the car. Instead of stopping, the social worker told Amber that her mom hadn't shown up and then simply drove right past her awaiting mother.

The last in-person visit Amber had with her mother was when she was about nine years old. Her mother had written a letter with a photo of herself to give to Amber. Evillene read the letter to Amber and then promptly threw them both out. To this day, Amber wishes she had that letter and photo of her mother. She cannot remember what it said.

Then, sadly, when Amber was twelve years old and in grade 6, her mother passed away from complications of her addictions. Amber's father had been in and out of prison and she didn't see him much. Amber misses her mother dearly and visits her grave on the anniversary of her death.

Growing up in foster care

Amber's recollection of growing up in foster care was rigid, unloving and punitive. In Amber's words, she recalls Evillene forcing her to take 'anger management' pills. She felt this was Evillene's way of controlling her. To this day, Amber doesn't know what the drug was. Evillene also insisted the girls joined cadets. Amber's cadet friends also participated in biathlon, so Amber joined that on her own accord.

That said, some of the things Amber's foster mother did do for her was appreciated. As an example, she created photo album keepsakes for both Amber and her sister. Amber cherishes those photos and has shared many of them with me.

Despite her home life, Amber was good in school, achieving honours and the adoration of all of her teachers. She was kind, quiet, respectful, and constantly helping others. These character traits still shine brightly today.

Amber lived with Evillene until she was fourteen years old, and all the foster kids were about one year apart. "Once they hit adolescence and started to voice opinions of their own, they all got kicked out, one by one," Amber bluntly affirmed. "We could never tell our social worker what was going on because we were only allowed to see her for five minutes at a time."

When Amber's sister was told to leave the foster home, she was sent to live in a different foster home. Amber's sister became pregnant, at the age of fifteen, and Evillene, in disagreement to the teenage pregnancy, kept Amber from visiting her. Evillene also forced an IUD birth control device on Amber as a result, which was very invasive, in Amber's words.

Amber had a mentor who was a male RCMP officer. His son was in cadets and Amber had made friends with him. Evillene didn't like Amber making friends and would get angry every time Amber went to his house. The RCMP officer knew this and told Amber if she ever needed a ride to cadets or biathlon, he would gladly pick her up. This is when Amber started talking to other people about what was going on at home and how hard it was. He was an excellent mentor and she was close with him for three years.

Tragically, Amber experienced another heartbreaking loss when her RCMP mentor was killed in the line of duty. Amber clearly remembers the day he was killed. Evillene had refused to drive her into Edmonton to watch a movie with her pregnant sister. Amber trekked the 90-minute walk from her house to the movie theatres. Almost at her destination, she passed the nearby Casino. The RCMP had blocked off a crime scene. Later that evening, after she had walked back home, Evillene told Amber her RCMP mentor had been murdered.

One Monday morning, after having spent the weekend in Canmore competing in biathlon provincials, Amber went to school only to find that all of her possessions had been left in the school office. She matter-of-factly stated to me, "Evillene threw me out because I'm old enough now to have my own opinions. I've shared what really went on in my foster home with my social worker."

CFS placed Amber with a new foster family. Amber told me her new foster family made it compulsory for her to be in her bedroom all the time. "It felt like a dungeon," Amber said flatly. After a week, Amber, fed up, ran away to her pregnant sister's foster home. They let her stay there for three months, and Amber was present when her nephew was born. Five months later, the girls fled to the city with the baby.

Once in Edmonton, Amber and her sister stayed with a friend of their mother's, who they referred to as their 'street mom.' There were many kids in their street mom's two-bedroom apartment. Authorities eventually intervened and relocated Amber to a group home. She was miserable and wanted to be with the people she loved. "The cops always said it was a safe place for me to live," Amber told me, but she kept running back to her street mom's apartment.

Amber tried drugs for the first time with an acquaintance on her way back to the group home. "You try doing meth and not get addicted to it," Amber had once said to me. She sold drugs for the first time when a random girl on social media asked if anyone had drugs. From there, things only got worse.

"When one comes, they all come," Amber said. "If you had drugs, you obviously had friends. I did a lot of crime because I needed money for drugs," Amber admitted.

"I don't remember what my first charge was, but I'm pretty sure it was shoplifting cheese and candles," she laughed. "Every time I got arrested, I was either drunk or high." She was never arrested while sober and she's still shocked she never got an impaired charge.

"I took the fall for a lot of crimes because I was young, female, and they let me off easy. The cops acted like they knew me, but really, they were racist and rude," Amber relayed. "They pretended to know me and they harassed me. They would call me over for nothing just to make me miss my bus," she said dismally.

Our early days

I was earning Amber's trust a little at a time. Her youth worker helped me connect with her on social media and I believe she enjoyed seeing me because of Hershey. About nine months after first meeting Amber, she was arrested for fleeing from the police while driving a stolen truck. She had been so frightened during the high-speed police chase that she had soiled herself. Hershey and I went to see her while she was waiting in a holding cell for a bail hearing. As soon as I opened the cell door, she looked up at me and broke into tears. With open arms, she ran toward me with a hug that I will never forget. We embraced for a long time. Amber was scared and alone. She was embarrassed, humiliated, and exhausted from her traumatic and chaotic life. She had hit rock bottom.

Amber was sentenced to the young offender centre for three months. It was the best thing that could have happened to her at that moment. Up until that point, she had always been released from custody; even to her surprise. Her genuine personality and radiant beauty affected everyone who attempted to say 'no' to her; police, lawyers, and even the justice of the peace. Until now. But Amber finally had the opportunity she needed, and desired, to plan and work toward the future she dreamed of. Two weeks prior to her release, surprisingly, Amber requested a new foster family.

A Growing Bond

A bond grew between Amber and me. Having decided to fully commit to mentoring Amber, now sixteen, I approached a family who lived outside of the city and who were looking to foster a teenage girl. Amber agreed to meet with them.

Naturally, and rightfully so, Amber was paralyzingly anxious about living with a new foster family but this foster family was different. They were excited to have Amber live with them and couldn't wait to meet her. They were friendly and loving. After the ten minutes in the car, the new foster mom walked out onto their front deck, beckoning to Amber and me, with a big smile on her face, "Well are y'all comin' in, 'er what?"

I assured Amber I would remain with her for the rest of the day, just in case she did not want to stay. I'd told her we would assess how she felt at the end of the night and that if she wanted to leave, she would be free to do so. She agreed to give it a try.

The new foster family had two dogs, a cat, a turtle, a parrot, and a brood of fuzzy baby chicks. Amber fondly referred to this foster family as the "Zoo Family." The Zoo Family and their animals helped make Amber feel welcome and safe. She wanted to stay.

Amber's sixteenth birthday had been a few days before her arrival, and knowing this, the Zoo Family had made her a birthday cake. We sang Happy Birthday and Amber cried. She was lonely. The acreage was a 45-minute drive from any civilization she was familiar with. The one thing that immediately helped Amber to feel welcome was that the Zoo

Family was very interested in learning about Indigenous culture. They asked Amber to teach them how to smudge (a cleansing smoke bath), which is a First Nations' tradition. She also taught her new family how to make bannock, an Indigenous type of fried bread. The Zoo Family especially liked playing music and drums and asked Amber to teach them dances. They laughed and had fun together. Amber was finally in a safe place to heal from many years of ongoing trauma.

Amber helped around the house with chores and one of them was taking care of the chicks. It wasn't until a few years later that Amber humorously admitted how much she dislikes chickens.

The Horse Ranch
As much as Amber enjoyed spending time with the Zoo Family and the animals, she desperately missed her biological family, friends, and the city. Amber was wanting to visit the city often, but we all knew she was not stable enough to return to that environment. Nonetheless, the Zoo Family understood Amber's longing for her sisters and street mom, so they arranged a trip to the city for Amber to visit family while the Zoo Family ran a few errands of their own.

During this visit, Amber and her sister got high. When the Zoo Family returned, Amber didn't want to leave her sister. The Zoo Family called me for help. Upon my arrival, Amber's street mom screeched at me, "Do you think this is a game, Constable Val?! This is life or death! Amber can *not* be here. She is not allowed to use alcohol or drugs in my home. I am helping to raise Amber's nephew and she is a bad influence!" Amber's street mom continued to roar. "Amber will not listen to me. You must keep her out of the city if she is going to survive."

I couldn't remember the last time someone had given me a good thrashing like that, but it was what Amber and everyone who cared about her needed to hear. It was painful to Amber's soul to hear those words; she loves her nephew dearly and desperately wanted to be a good auntie.

I'd learned my lesson. From here on, no meant no. I ramped up my tough love, took her phone away, and then sat down with my husband, who is Métis, to brainstorm what else we could do.

"Familiarize her with some horses; they are a First Nation's icon," he said. "An elderly friend of mine owns a horse ranch. He has five pregnant mares and three new foals," he continued. "He is very busy and could use some help taking care of them."

I called my husband's friend to ask him if he would be open to having Amber as a volunteer. He was delighted to give her a chance, and very happy to have the extra help. I then went to the Zoo Family home to ask Amber if she liked horses.

She smiled, "Yes, why?"

Relieved, I said, "Get in!" as I motioned to my vehicle. "We're goin' for a drive." Amber hopped in, along with her foster father, and away we went.

The horse ranch was beautiful and could accommodate hundreds of horses. Amber was absolutely captivated by the mares, but even more so by the foals. The horse owner then explained to Amber how he could use some help, if she were interested in volunteering at his ranch. Her foster father offered to drive her to the ranch every day and Amber happily accepted. She couldn't wait to start.

It was obvious to the Zoo Family and me that this horse ranch provided an earnest, uncomplicated and unconditional form of love and affection for Amber. It was a positive and healthy place for Amber to learn new skills. The reciprocity of love was exactly what Amber, and the foals, needed. The horses had a profound effect on Amber, and this arrangement was both cathartic and rewarding. She did a lot of chores and said the new routine had helped her start a healthy lifestyle. It was a lot of work shovelling all those 'code browns,' as she called them (horse droppings), but she was happy to do it. She knew the horses needed her help. The owner named one of the newborn fillies after Amber with the name Kosawin, a Cree name meaning jewel.

In addition to Amber's work at the ranch, I introduced Amber to a volunteer who was, and remains, very engaged with Indigenous culture. She and Amber sewed skirts together and went to pow wows and round dances. At this time, I had known Amber for just over a year. It never occurred to me until then that she was very connected to aspects of her ancestral culture. Cops really only get to see one side of the coin when they deal with individuals and it was an honour getting to know this other side of Amber.

Despite Amber's love for the horses and cultural outings, after three months she was still longing to be reunited with her siblings. The Zoo Family and I had concerns; we didn't think she was ready to move back into the city yet. Amber insisted she was. She had proven herself on the horse ranch, discontinued contact with harmful friends, and was now substance-free. She sought to steer her own ship without the support of a foster family. She was still very young to be venturing out all on her own, however, so her social worker found a supervised apartment building in the city. We all crossed our fingers and hoped for the best. It's all we could do.

Thankfully, Amber exceeded our expectations. She acquired a full-time job, rebuilt relationships with her family and friends, and was proud of herself for only using substances socially. Amber stayed in touch with me regularly, visited the Zoo Family often, and even brought her nephew out for a ride on one of the horses. She believes the key to chartering her success was having a large, supportive team behind her.

The therapy animals, her determination to become healthy, and her desire to visit with her nephew were all motivating factors for her improvement. It was Hershey, however, who first cracked open that gate for her. As she acknowledged me later on, "I had a lot to say, but I was too afraid to talk to the police. Having Hershey there helped reduce my fear so I could talk."

Amber ~ present day
I am continually impressed with Amber; who she's become and all she's achieved. I've heard say that if you help one person, you help seven. Amber is helping more than seven people; she now mentors her siblings, cousins, nephews and friends. Last year, Amber worked hard to earn her high school diploma.

When Amber and her life partner welcomed a child of their own, the Zoo Family hosted a joyous party to celebrate. They made all of her favourite treats, in special shapes showcasing her Indigenous heritage: teepee ice cream cones, bird-nest cupcakes, feather marshmallows, and even an owl-shaped fruit platter!

Amber's resilience along with her focussed goals allowed these special people to help save her life. The Zoo Family embraced Amber's culture and put her — a teenager — in charge of teaching adults something. They knew Amber had had her culture stripped from her, and that taking away someone's culture removes who that person is as a whole.

Through embracing and celebrating her heritage, the Zoo Family honoured who Amber is, providing a space for her to manifest her power back. Amber and the Zoo Family were also able to facilitate Amber's connectiveness and took in her younger sister... but that's another story for another day, folks.

Me ~ present day

AMBER: Empowered >> Educated >> Substance-free >> Proud and Loving Momma >> Breaking Intergenerational Trauma >> Driver >> Employee >> Mentor

VAL: Humbled >> Open >> Listening >> Understanding >> Re-educated >> Empathetic >> Helpful >> Mentor

Many of the highly-traumatized adolescents whom I've worked with in Youth Unit had a profound effect on me; how could they not? I became a judgment-free police officer and was more attentive to what these young people had to say and needed. The biggest difference I noticed within myself was that I stopped labeling people. An 'addict' became 'a person who struggles with addictions.' A 'homeless person' transitioned into 'a person with more complex issues than their housing.' This reframing is important, both in helping those who suffer and in helping us to provide adequate care.

When my tenure came to an end within my specialized area, an empathetic social worker discerningly (and accurately) predicted, "Once you work with high-risk youth, you will never want to stop."

He was right. And I didn't stop. In fact, working with traumatized youth had been an education unlike any other, and it was time to put that education to good use. Once back in uniform, I pondered how I was going to use this acquired knowledge to help the public more broadly. For the first time in my career, despite my twenty-nine years of service, I initially feared the judgment would be flipped back onto me. But this old dog had learned some new tricks…

I now find myself in the last posting of my career as a member of The Human-centered Engagement Liaison Partnership Unit — or 'HELP'. I now have the time to build relationships with those who need it most. Hopefully, this will be the start of bigger changes and more divisions like the HELP Unit will expand to be common among other police agencies across Canada. When possible, it is important for the police to help remove blame and shame. Sometimes we can't, of course, but if we had more police specialized units built around the philosophy of this relationship building, it may allow for better treatment of each other.

When I retire next year, I am planning to travel across Canada, with my hairy, pad-footed partner, to read Hershey's books to children. However, something Amber said to me a few weeks ago has me feeling somewhat trepidatious about retiring from the police service. She said, "You play a big role for me to kick ass in life."

I find myself wondering now if I will be as kick-ass a civilian mentor as I am a police mentor. Upon retirement, I will again become a civilian — something I haven't been since I was nineteen years old. My entire professional career, my adult life, and my authoritative powers, have all been molded by the clothing and accoutrements I wear while on duty. It may seem strange to non-officers, but the police uniform does provide an extra layer of confidence, status and purpose; without the 'working suit' I've become so used to presenting myself in, will people view me differently? Do I know who I am or how to work without it? Only time will tell.

AFTERWORD

Dr. J. Thomas Dalby

I JOINED THE Forensic Unit at the Calgary General Hospital in 1982. This was the first such unit in a Canadian general hospital and our purpose was to evaluate individuals displaying symptoms of a mental disorder when they appeared in court on criminal charges. That initiation into the criminal justice system brought me into direct contact with many police officers and over the years since I have provided treatment services to police officers, worked on investigations with them, helped select officers for special internal duties as well as international service, formally taught them in university courses and seminars and presented court evidence for them when they had faced disciplinary charges in the line of their duties. Over four decades, I have come to know what these dedicated men and women face not only in their direct service but the burden we ask them to carry for us — sometimes for the rest of their lives.

Officers would describe in detail seeing lifeless bodies of little kids, knowing another human had cruelly taken their barely begun lives.

The stories in this volume reveal the complexity of police work. Not everyone is suited to this demanding, stressful and occasionally dangerous job. To even become a police officer requires clearing many hurdles — interviews, background checks, psychological test batteries, physical evaluations, polygraphs, cadet training and more. Those that become police officers will pay a price for their vocational choice — they begin to understand this after a few years of service. When I provided treatment services to officers, I would call this the 13th year cliff — the officer had weathered the storm for that long, but retirement was still a long way off and the accumulating stresses were becoming overwhelming.

There are many sources of police stress. The most obvious is *occupational stress* — rotating work shifts are common, and most officers work more than 45 hours a week and struggle to get their work done, often taking some home with them. They also encounter situations that the public cannot imagine. I was once treating an officer from a northern isolated posting and he carried a big shovel and green garbage bags in the trunk of his cruiser — the purpose of these was for scooping up body parts from fatal accidents —not a usual expectation for a cop in the city but there was no one else to do this gruesome work up north. Officers would describe in detail seeing the lifeless bodies of little kids, some made worse knowing another human had cruelly taken their barely begun lives.

What happens when police experience these stressors from all sides? The first thing to go is work/life balance.

The brutal reality of life for many people is made very apparent to police officers every day as they view the underbelly of human nature. Most officers accept this going in and say that *organizational stress* is more troubling to them than the actual tasks. Regardless of their on-the-job performances there is little room for advancement in many law enforcement agencies, little recognition is given of their diligent effort and there are endless clerical tasks which if not done right could torpedo an important case. Most police organizations inherited a quasi-military hierarchy to go along with military style uniforms, but perceived support or even perceived leadership can be minimal. Officers are given lots of discretion for making decisions in the community but if things go wrong can they count on support from the top? Police are trained in use-of-force and are enabled by law to use force but guidelines for this are very ambiguous. Typically, only they know what the real situation they were facing was like when making a split-second decision to protect themselves. Police also have *criminal justice stressors* — days and months have been spent collecting evidence on a case, yet court decisions may not go in their favor even when they have done everything exactly as they should have. Police officers often develop a feeling that different rules apply to different people. They can run into a repeat offender on the street after successfully contributing to their conviction and released early back into the community to continue their antisocial ways. Finally, there are *public stressors* — the newspaper account of their cases may be distorted or missing important facts and many such reports are often perceived as derogatory by officers. They are frustrated that social agencies have not done their part in assisting the needy and many tasks of police officers are rightly the responsibility of other agencies. No police force in Canada needs to be 'defunded' but proper funding of other agencies needs to be examined.

What happens when police experience these stressors from all sides? The first thing to go is work/life balance. About 85 per cent of police officers are married and most have children. Almost half of police officers indicate that their work interferes with their family life on a regular basis. While required to keep in good physical shape, after an exhausting work schedule, most claim they are fatigued and don't have to time to maintain their physical health. It is not just the lack of exercise, but stress also induces many physical illnesses — high blood pressure, cardiovascular disease and many others. Of course, mental health is just as precarious, and many policemen and policewomen struggle with depressed mood, PTSD and alcohol abuse. PTSD is a real entity — physical and mental — and requires specialized treatment. I saw one officer two days after a traumatic incident — he was speeding to get to a domestic dispute involving a firearm in a rural location and an elderly woman was backing out of her driveway lined with hedges and did not hear the cruiser's siren. The resulting crash killed the woman instantly and the 'what if's' dominated the officer's mind, and it was months before the images of the accident diminished. In prior generations, police officers resisted being 'shrunk' but this stigma has become less of an obstacle and most forces have resident psychologists. One of the best interventions for trauma is peer support and these types of arrangements are now common.

Is this a profession you would want your child to aspire to? It quickly became clear to me early on that law enforcement attracts some of the best citizens we have, and research shows this — they are honest, stable, responsible, have a sense of humour (vital in most officers), good team players, show high motivation and possess keen problem-solving skills. The job itself and the multiple stressors I have cited will challenge all these traits that we value in them. Like all professions, there are those that should not be police officers, but this is a very small proportion of the police population.

Canada (Toronto) organized the first professional police force in North America in 1834 just five years after the birth of the Metropolitan London police and was modelled on that early force. When I assisted in the selection of police officers to serve in international forces, it was with satisfaction to see that Canadians were highly valued and frequently were placed in charge of groups of officers from many other countries. These officers were unarmed in many of these duties but their demeanor of respect and cooperation with local citizens gained them much praise and negotiation and mediation were their tools.

Hopefully, the reader of these interesting stories from a selection of both male and female officers, will recognize the humanness of their characters. We ask a lot and even expect perfection from officers when this is never possible. A true appreciation of their dedication and passion should be the result.

— Dr. J. Thomas Dalby *PhD R. Psych., ABN, 2021*

Dr. Dalby is a psychologist who has been in practice for 43 years and specializes in forensic psychology and neuropsychology. He held appointments with the faculties of social science and medicine at the University of Calgary for 33 years and remains affiliated with Athabasca University and has been since 1977. He is the author of over 120 articles and books in law, psychology and medicine.

ACKNOWLEDGEMENTS

Debbie J. Doyle

As with all things in life, others help us, guide us and provide support: we do not walk alone.

First and foremost, I would like to thank Dr. Lorene Shyba and Durvile Publications. This book would not have been written if it was not for you, your patience and expertise.

I want to recognize all of the authors. Your willingness to share your stories with the rest of society shows that you joined the police to help others. You continue to do so by sharing moments from your past and present, revealing your weaknesses, struggles and suffering, but also your triumphs and ability to adapt and overcome. Thank you for agreeing to work with me on this project.

I want to thank all of you who were interested in contributing but were unable to do so. I especially appreciate your honesty during our phone and email conversations. Sometimes wounds are too deep to fully heal.

Thank you to Sherri Zickefoose and Dr. J. Thomas Dalby. Your contributions to this book provide unique insights into the actions and minds of police.

For the survivors, otherwise known by some as victims. We wish we didn't have to deal with you because then you would never have been hurt. Your pain and suffering are not lost on us. We carry it until the day we are laid to rest. I am awed at your resilience, strength and forgiveness. We always want to help people and you are the reason we became police officers.

To everyone who reads this book. Democratic policing is not dictated by autocrats and demigods, but by society. You have allowed police officers into your communities and as times change, society does, and so much policing. I challenge you to pick up a pair of glasses and not view the whole of policing, but individual police officers through a lens of humanity. They are your brothers and sisters, neighbours, hockey and baseball coaches, even your church organists. They were like you before they donned the uniform and are still like you after they removed it for the last time. As you read each chapter in this book, you will realize that each of us has been affected by the career we eagerly chose.

A special thanks to Suzi Meyers. As always, Gerry's photographs inspire. We miss him.

For my friends and family. I appreciate your understanding when I couldn't make lunch or coffee dates because I was too engrossed with compiling this book. And when I did and was in the room with you, I apologize that my mind was not.

To my parents, Bill and Lil Laiss. Without your patience, guidance and love, I would not have become the woman I am today. You taught me that there are no boundaries for what women can do and accomplish. You ensured my childhood focused on education but also sports and music. I'm absolutely sure that all accordion players go to heaven. Thank you for your perseverance in raising me and supporting me to follow my dreams.

And to my husband, Dan Doyle. I cannot imagine working on this project or anything else without your support. Your patience is that of a six-point white-tail deer. And yes, 2 a.m. is the new 10 p.m. — I'm sure of it. You are, as always, brutally honest with me, and that honesty has forced me to do better in every aspect of my life. You taught me to listen to not merely what is said, but what isn't. You have shown me that what is seen may not necessarily be what has occurred. And the sound of your voice always brings a smile to my face. We are the lucky ones because we help each other with the wounds of policing. You have brought me into the light from the darkness and are the angel on my shoulder, constantly adjusting my compass when it veers off course. You are my Yang.

DURVILE TRUE CASES SERIES

∎ ∎ ∎

Tough Crimes: True Cases by Top Canadian Criminal Lawyers
By Edward L. Greenspan et al
Book 1 in the True Cases Series

"Tough Crimes demonstrates that Crown prosecutors and criminal defence lawyers do not escape unscathed from serious trials. The disturbing memories remain."
— Hon. John C. Major, CC QC, Justice, Supreme Court of Canada.

Tough Crimes is a collection of thoughtful and insightful essays from some of Canada's most prominent criminal lawyers. Stories include wrongful convictions, reasonable doubt, homicides, and community spirit.
Edited by C.D. Evans and Lorene Shyba

Price: $29.95, 24.95 US
Paperback 288 pages

ISBN: 978-0-9689754-6-6 (2014)

Also available as ebook and audiobook

Shrunk: Crime and Disorders of the Mind
True Cases by Forensic Experts
By J. Thomas Dalby et al
Book 2 in the True Cases Series

"The workings of the criminally disordered minds has always been a fascinating subject. Does our prison system throw away the key after incarceration, or is it worthwhile to rehabilitate?"
— Earl Levy, QC

SHRUNK is a collection of true cases by eminent Canadian and international forensic psychologists and psychiatrists facing the tough topic of mental illness in the criminal justice system.
Edited by Lorene Shyba and J. Thomas Dalby
Foreword by Dr. Lisa Ramshaw

Price: $29.95, 24.95 US
Paperback 272 pages

ISBN: 978-0-9947352-0-1 (2016)

Also available as ebook and audiobook

DURVILE TRUE CASES SERIES

■ ■ ■

More Tough Crimes:
True Cases by Canadian Judges
and Criminal Lawyers
By Donald Bayne *et al*
Book 3 in the True Cases Series

Women in Criminal Justice:
True Cases By and About
Canadian Women and the Law
By Hon. Susan Lang *et al*
Book 4 in the True Cases Series

"A revealing, at times searing and always very human look inside our criminal courtrooms and the people who populate them."
— Sean Fine, *The Globe and Mail*

"The reader emerges with pictures in mind ... women working without respite to achieve just outcomes for the people they deal with often in the face of difficulty."
— Rt. Hon. Beverley McLachlin

The third book in the "True Cases" series, *More Tough Crimes* provides readers with a window into the insightful thinking of some of Canada's best legal minds from coast to coast.

Stories in *Women in Criminal Justice* deal with terrorism, drugs, sexual assault, mental disorders, motherhood, LGBTQ+, Indigenous, and other urgent issues of our time.

Edited by William Trudell & Lorene Shyba
Foreword by Hon. Patrick LeSage

Edited by William Trudell & Lorene Shyba
Foreword by Rt. Hon. Beverley McLachlin

Price: $29.95, 24.95 US
Paperback 272 pages

Price: $29.95, 24.95 US
Paperback 272 pages

ISBN: 978-0-9947352-5-6 (2017)

ISBN: 978-0-9947352-4-9 (2018)

Also available as ebook and audiobook

Also available as ebook and audiobook

DURVILE TRUE CASES SERIES

■ ■ ■

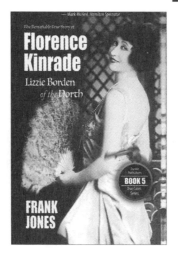
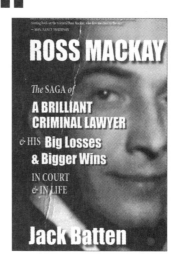

Florence Kinrade:
Lizzie Borden of the North
By Frank Jones
Book 5 in the True Cases Series

"Frank Jones has always had a knack for finding the quirkiest and most interesting true crime tales, and relating them with the skill you'd expect from a lifelong, first rate journalist, and this latest is no exception."
— Linwood Barclay, Author

In 1909, Florence Kinrade is a dutiful daughter, engaged to the parson's son. She also leads a double life as a vaudeville showgirl in Richmond, Virginia. Florence becomes the central figure in a gruesome crime.

Price: $29.95, 24.95 US
Paperback 272 pages

ISBN: 9781988824352 (2019)

Also available as ebook and audiobook

Ross Mackay, The Saga of a
Brilliant Criminal Lawyer
By Jack Batten
Book 6 in the True Cases Series

"When tragedy hits the gifted, the loss is hard to explain. But Jack Batten succeeds. He marries journalism and law, meticulous fact-driven research, to give us this riveting book on the talented Ross Mackay, who flew too close to the sun."
—Hon. Nancy Morrison, Former Justice of the Supreme Court of B.C.

Ross Mackay was the counsel for the accused in the trials of the last men to be hanged in Canada. He was a mere thirty years old when he lost both clients to the gallows.

Price: $35.00, 29.95 US
Paperback 288 pages

ISBN: 978-1-988824-34-5 (2020)

Also available as ebook and audiobook

DURVILE TRUE CASES SERIES

■ ■ ■

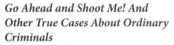

Go Ahead and Shoot Me! And Other True Cases About Ordinary Criminals
By Doug Heckbert
Book 7 in the True Cases Series

"I'm struck by how the True Cases series has a multiplicity of authentic perspectives that are able to be our proxy or conduit into amazing worlds. Go Ahead and Shoot Me! are stories that are happening in our community and to our neighbours that we should know about but don't."
—Grant Stovers, CKUA Radio

Go Ahead and Shoot Me! is a collection of stories written by a former probation officer about real people who have been convicted of real crimes.

Price: $35.00, 29.95 US
Paperback 288 pages

ISBN: 978-1-988824-34-5 (2020)

Also available as ebook and audiobook

After the Force: True Cases and Investigations by Law Enforcement Officers
Edited by Det. Debbie J. Doyle (ret)
Book 8 in the True Cases Series

After the Force features true cases and investigations, this time by Canadian police officers who have served in municipal, provincial and federal police services. Stories in this anthology are by people who have been passionate about their work in law enforcement and who generously explain what it was about their work that led them to choose a career or specific way of life "after the force."

Price: $35.00, 29.95 US
Paperback 272 pages

ISBN: 978-1-988824-49-9 (2021)

Also available as ebook and audiobook

 Durvile.com

Books in the UpRoute Spirit of Nature Series
Series Editors: Raymond Yakeleya and Lorene Shyba

The Tree by the Woodpile and Other Dene Spirit of Nature Tales
Raymond Yakeleya
Illustrations: Deborah Desmarais

978-1-988824-03-1 *(pbk)* | 978-1-988824-52-9 *(audiobook)*
978-1-988824-16-1 *(e-book)*

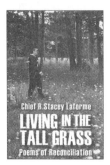

Living in the Tall Grass: Poems of Reconciliation
Chief R. Stacey Laforme

978-1-988824-05-5 *(pbk)* | 978-1-988824-32-1 *(audiobook)*
978-0-968975-49-7 *(e-book)*

Lillian & Kokomis: The Spirit of Dance
Lynda Partridge
Foreword: Chief R. Stacey Laforme
Illustrations: Dave Nicholson

978-1-988824-27-7 *(pbk)* | 978-1-988824-29-1 *(audiobook)*
978-1-988824-28-4 *(e-book)*

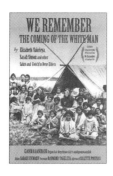

We Remember the Coming of the White Man, First Edition
Authors: Elizabeth Yakeleya, Sarah Simon *et al*
Editor: Sarah Stewart
Foreword: Raymond Yakeleya

978-1-988824-24-6 *(pbk)* | 978-1-988824-37-6 *(audiobook)*
978-1-988824-56-7 *(e-book)*

We Remember the Coming of the White Man, Special Edition
Editors: Sarah Stewart & Raymond Yakeleya

978-1-988824-63-5 *(pbk)* | 978-1-988824-74-1 *(audiobook)*
978-1-988824-75-8 *(e-book)*

Stories of Métis Women: Tales My Kookum Told Me
Bailey Oster & Marilyn Lizee
Foreword: Audrey Poitras

978-1-988824-21-5 *(pbk)* | 978-1-988824-69-7 *(audiobook)*
978-1-98882-46-8-0 *(e-book)*

Îethka Nakoda Language in Îethka Nakoda Country
Îethka Îabi ne Îethka Mâkochi nen
Editor: Trent Fox. Authors: Valentina Fox, Trudy Wesley, Natasha Wesley, Glenda Crawler, Trent Fox
Illustrations: Tanisha Wesley
978-1-988824-73-4 *(pbk)* | 978-1-988824-58-1 *(audio)*
978-1-988824-80-2 *(e-book)*

AFTER THE FORCE